(don't)

^GO TO HELL

by Jan Y. Cliff

Reform Publisher

Come, ye children, hearken unto me: I will teach
you the *fear* of the LORD.
(Psalm 34:11)

Q. & A.

Q:
You may be asking yourself some or all of the following questions:

What the **HELL** is this book about?
What the **HELL** is the author trying to prove?
Why the **HELL** should I waste my time and money to buy and read this book?
Why the **HELL** are there so many duplicate verses?
Who the **HELL** are you, or anyone else for that matter, to tell me what to do?

A:
This book is designed as a scare tactic;
TO SCARE THE HELL OUT OF YOU!

Soli Deo Gloria!
JYC

Forward

Jesus Christ was the kindest, most humble and approachable man who ever lived. No man or woman in history has been more loving and kind than Jesus. **YET, it was He (in the Gospels and the Revelation) who spoke more forthrightly and clearly on the subject of Eternal Punishment than any man!** No Prophet, Lawgiver or Apostle ever taught the subject of Everlasting Punishment more than Jesus of Nazareth.

While being faithful to His warnings, we must also proclaim that God does not want anyone to perish, but all to come to repentance. (2 Peter 3:9) When the Bible says that, "God so loved the world," (John 3:16) the word includes everyone reading these pages. He gave His one and only Son so that ALL who confess their sins to him and invite Christ into his/her life, will find forgiveness and eternal life. God loves you in this manner.

Whatever else you many accomplish during your earthly life, be certain above all else that Jesus is in your heart and that you will not be separated from God in eternity. *Nothing can be greater than Eternal Life.* **Nothing will be more terrifying than Eternal Punishment!** Choose Christ and life this very moment.

Bishop Roi Herald

CONTENTS

Chapter 1: HELL   p.5
Chapter 2: FURNACE OF FIRE   p.12
Chapter 3: BRIMSTONE   p.14
Chapter 4: TORMENT   p.18
Chapter 5: DARKNESS   p.26
Chapter 6: LAKE OF FIRE   p.35
Chapter 7: INDIGNATION   p.37
Chapter 8: EVERLASTING   p.39
Chapter 9: CONDEMN   p.41
Chapter 10: CORRUPTION   p.48
Chapter 11: DESTROY   p.53
Chapter 12: CURSED   p.60
Chapter 13: UNQUENCHABLE FIRE   p.62
Chapter 14: DAMNATION   p.63
Chapter 15: DEATH   p.68
Chapter 16: FEAR   p.79
Chapter 17: PERISH   p.98
Chapter 18: GUILTY   p.105
Chapter 19: PUNISHMENT   p.108
Chapter 20: VENGEANCE   p.110
Chapter 21: FIRE   p.113
Chapter 22: WRATH   p.138
Chapter 23: BURN   p.155
Chapter 24: FLAME   p.162
Chapter 25: BLACK   p.165
Chapter 26: SCORCH   p.167
Chapter 27: WORM DIETH NOT   p.169
Chapter 28: JUDGEMENT   p.170
Chapter 29: PERDITION   p.198
Chapter 30: BEWARE   p.202
Chapter 31: **REPENT**   p.206
Chapter 32: **STRIVE**   p.219
Chapter 33: **TURN**   p.220
Chapter 34: **TAKE HEED**   p.222
Chapter 35: **SAVED**   p.227
Chapter 36: **SALVATION**   p.242
Chapter 37: **EVERLASTING LIFE**   p.255
Chapter 38: **ETERNAL LIFE**   p.260
Chapter 39: **PARADISE**   p.274
Chapter 40: **VICTORY**   p.275

Chapter 1

HELL

Ye have heard that it was said of them of old time, Thou shalt not kill; and whosoever shall kill shall be in danger of the judgment: But I say unto you, That whosoever is angry with his brother without a cause shall be in danger of ***the judgment***: and whosoever shall say to his brother, Raca, shall be in danger of the council: but whosoever shall say, Thou fool, shall be in danger of **HELL** fire. Therefore if thou bring thy gift to the altar, and there rememberest that thy brother hath ought against thee; Leave there thy gift before the altar, and go thy way; *first be reconciled to thy brother,* and then come and offer thy gift. Agree with thine adversary quickly, whiles thou art in the way with him; lest at any time the adversary deliver thee to the judge, and the judge deliver thee to the officer, and thou be cast into prison. Verily I say unto thee, Thou shalt by no means come out thence, till thou hast paid the uttermost farthing. Ye have heard that it was said by them of old time, Thou shalt not commit adultery: But I say unto you, That whosoever looketh on a woman to lust after her hath committed adultery with her already in his heart. And if thy **right eye** offend thee, *pluck it out,* and cast it from thee: for it is profitable for thee that one of thy members should perish, and not that thy whole body should be cast into **HELL**. And if thy right **hand** offend thee, *cut it off,* and cast it from thee: for it is profitable for thee that one of thy members should perish, and not that thy whole body should be cast into **HELL**. (Matthew 5:21-30)

And fear not them which kill the body, but are not able to kill the soul: but rather *fear him which is able to destroy both soul and body in* **HELL**. (Matthew10:28)

Then began he to **upbraid the cities** wherein most of his mighty works were done, because they repented not: Woe unto thee, Chorazin! woe unto thee, Bethsaida! for if the mighty works, which were done in you, had been done in Tyre and Sidon, they would have repented long ago in sackcloth and ashes. But I say unto you, It shall be more tolerable for Tyre and Sidon at the day of judgment, than for you. And thou, Capernaum, which art exalted unto heaven, shalt be brought down to **HELL**: for if the mighty works, which have been done in thee, had been done in Sodom, it would have remained until this day. But I say unto you, That **it shall be more tolerable for the land of Sodom in the day of judgment, than for thee.** (Matthew 11:20-24)

But whoso shall **offend** one of these little ones which believe in me, it were better for him that a millstone were hanged about his neck, and that he were drowned in the depth of the sea. Woe unto the world because of offences! for it must needs be that offences come; but woe to that man by whom the offence cometh. Wherefore if thy hand or thy foot offend thee, cut them off, and cast them from thee: it is better for thee to enter into life halt or maimed, rather than having two hands or two feet to be cast into everlasting fire. And if thine eye offend thee, pluck it out, and cast it from thee: it is better for thee to enter into life with one eye, rather than having two eyes to be **cast into HELL fire.** (Matthew 18:6-9)

But he that is *greatest* among you shall be your *servant*. And whosoever shall exalt himself shall be abased; and he that shall *humble himself* shall be exalted. But woe unto you, scribes and Pharisees, hypocrites! for ye shut up the kingdom of heaven against men: for ye neither go in yourselves, neither suffer ye them that are entering to go in. Woe unto you, scribes and Pharisees, hypocrites! for ye devour widows' houses, and for a pretence make long prayer: therefore **ye shall receive the greater damnation.** Woe unto you, scribes and Pharisees, hypocrites! for ye compass sea and land to make one proselyte, and when he is made, ye make him twofold more the child of **HELL** than yourselves. (Matthew 23:11-15)

Woe unto you, scribes and Pharisees, **hypocrites!** for ye are like unto whited sepulchres, which indeed appear beautiful outward, but are within full of dead men's bones, and of all uncleanness. Even so ye also outwardly appear righteous unto men, but within ye are full of hypocrisy and iniquity. Woe unto you, scribes and Pharisees, hypocrites! because ye build the tombs of the prophets, and garnish the sepulchres of the righteous, And say, If we had been in the days of our fathers, we would not have been partakers with them in the blood of the prophets. Wherefore ye be witnesses unto yourselves, that ye are the children of them which killed the prophets. Fill ye up then the measure of your fathers. Ye serpents, ye generation of vipers, **how can ye escape the damnation of HELL?** (Matthew 23:27-33)

And whosoever shall **offend** one of these little ones that believe in me, it is better for him that a millstone were hanged about his neck, and he were cast into the sea. And if thy hand offend thee, cut it off: it is better for thee to enter into life maimed, than having two hands to go into **HELL**, into the fire that never shall be quenched: Where their worm dieth not, and the fire is not quenched. And if thy foot offend thee, cut it off: it is better for thee to enter halt into life, than having two feet to be cast into **HELL**, into the fire that never shall be quenched: Where their worm dieth not, and the fire is not quenched. And if thine eye offend thee, pluck it out: it is better for thee to enter into the kingdom of God with one eye, than having two eyes to be **cast into HELL fire:** Where their worm dieth not, and the fire is not quenched. (Mark 9:42-48)

But into whatsoever city ye enter, and they receive you not, go your ways out into the streets of the same, and say, Even the very dust of your city, which cleaveth on us, we do wipe off against you: notwithstanding be ye sure of this, that the kingdom of God is come nigh unto you. But I say unto you, that it shall be more tolerable in that day for Sodom, than for that city. Woe unto thee, <u>Chorazin</u>! woe unto thee, <u>Bethsaida</u>! for if the mighty works had been done in Tyre and Sidon, which have been done in you, they had a great while ago *repented,* sitting in sackcloth and ashes. But it shall be more tolerable for Tyre and Sidon at the judgment, than for you. And thou, <u>Capernaum</u>, which art exalted to heaven, shalt be thrust down to **HELL**. *He that heareth you heareth me;* and <u>**he that despiseth you despiseth me; and he that despiseth me despiseth him that sent me.**</u> (Luke 10:10-16)

And I say unto you my friends, Be not afraid of them that kill the body, and after that have no more that they can do. But *I will forewarn you whom ye shall fear:* **Fear him, which after he hath killed hath power to cast into HELL**; yea, I say unto you, *Fear him.* (Luke 12:4-5)

There was a certain **rich man**, which was clothed in purple and fine linen, and fared sumptuously every day: And there was a certain ***beggar*** named Lazarus, which was laid at his gate, full of sores, And desiring to be fed with the crumbs which fell from the rich man's table: moreover the dogs came and licked his sores. And it came to pass, that the beggar died, and was carried by the angels into Abraham's bosom: the rich man also died, and was buried; And in **HELL** he lift up his eyes, being in torments, and seeth Abraham afar off, and Lazarus in his bosom. And he cried and said, Father Abraham, have mercy on me, and send Lazarus, that he may dip the tip of his finger in water, and cool my tongue; for I am tormented in this flame. But Abraham said, *Son, remember that thou in thy lifetime receivedst thy good things, and likewise Lazarus evil things: but* **now <u>he is comforted</u>, and <u>thou art tormented</u>.** (Luke 16:19-25)

But there were **false prophets** also among the people, even as there shall be **false teachers** among you, who privily shall bring in **<u>damnable heresies</u>**, even denying the Lord that bought them, and bring upon themselves swift destruction. And *many* shall follow their pernicious ways; by reason of whom the way of truth shall be evil spoken of. And through <u>covetousness</u> shall they with feigned words make merchandise of you: whose judgment now of a long time lingereth not, and their damnation slumbereth not. For if God spared not the angels that sinned, but cast them down to **HELL**, and delivered them into chains of darkness, to be reserved unto judgment; And spared not the old world, but saved Noah the eighth person, a preacher of righteousness, bringing in the flood upon the world of the ungodly; And turning the cities of Sodom and Gomorrha into ashes condemned them with an overthrow, <u>making them an **ensample** unto those that after should live ungodly</u>; And delivered just Lot, vexed with the filthy conversation of the wicked: (For that righteous man dwelling among them, in seeing and hearing, vexed his righteous soul from day to day with their unlawful deeds;) *The Lord knoweth how to deliver the **godly** out of temptations,* and **<u>to reserve the unjust unto the day of judgment to be punished</u>:** (2 Peter 2:1-9)

And in the midst of the seven candlesticks one like unto the **Son of man**, clothed with a garment down to the foot, and girt about the paps with a golden girdle. His head and his hairs were white like wool, as white as snow; and his eyes were as a flame of fire; And his feet like unto fine brass, as if they burned in a furnace; and his voice as the sound of many waters. And he had in his right hand seven stars: and out of his mouth went a sharp twoedged sword: and his countenance was as the sun shineth in his strength. And when I saw him, I fell at his feet as dead. And he laid his right hand upon me, saying unto me, *Fear not; I am the first and the last:* I am he that liveth, and was dead; and, behold, I am alive for evermore, Amen; and **have the keys of HELL and of death.** (Revelation 1:13-18)

And I saw a ***great white throne,*** and him that sat on it, from whose face the earth and the heaven fled away; and there was found no place for them. And *I saw the dead, small and great, stand before God*; and the books were opened: and another book was opened, which is the book of life: and the dead were judged out of those things which were written in the books, *according to their works*. And the sea gave up the dead which were in it; and death and **HELL** delivered up the dead which were in them: and they were **judged every man** *according to their works*. And death and **HELL** were cast into the lake of fire. This is the second death. And whosoever was *not* found written in the book of life was cast into the lake of fire. (Revelation 20:11-15)

Chapter 2

FURNACE OF FIRE

He answered and said unto them, He that soweth the good seed is the Son of man; The field is the world; the **good seed** are the children of the kingdom; but the **tares** are the children of the wicked one; The enemy that sowed them is the devil; the harvest is the end of the world; and the reapers are the angels. As therefore the **tares** <u>are gathered and burned in the</u> **FIRE**; so shall it be in the end of this world. The Son of man shall send forth his angels, and they shall gather out of his kingdom <u>all things that</u> **offend**, and <u>them which</u> ***do*** <u>**iniquity**</u>. And shall cast them into a **FURNACE OF FIRE**: there shall be wailing and gnashing of teeth. (Matthew 13:37-42)

Again, the kingdom of heaven is like unto ***a net***, that was cast into the sea, and gathered of every kind: Which, when it was full, they drew to shore, and sat down, and gathered the *good into vessels*, but <u>cast the bad away</u>. So shall it be at the end of the world: the angels shall come forth, and **<u>sever the wicked</u> from among *the just*,** And shall cast them into the **FURNACE OF FIRE**: there shall be wailing and gnashing of teeth. (Matthew 13:47-50)

And the <u>fifth angel</u> sounded, and I saw a star fall from heaven unto the earth: and to him was given the key of the <u>bottomless pit</u>. And he opened the bottomless pit; and there arose a smoke out of the pit, as the smoke of a great **FURNACE**; and the sun and the air were darkened by reason of the smoke of the pit. And there came out of the smoke **locusts** upon the earth: and unto them was given power, as the scorpions of the earth have power. And it was commanded them that they should not hurt the grass of the earth, neither any green thing, neither any tree; but <u>only those men which have *not* the seal of God in their foreheads</u>. And to them it was given that they should not kill them, but that they should be **tormented five months:** and their torment was as the <u>torment of a scorpion</u>, when he striketh a man. And in those days shall men seek death, and shall not find it; and shall desire to die, and death shall flee from them. (Revelation 9:1-6)

Chapter 3

BRIMSTONE

And as it was in the **days of Noe,** so shall it be also in the days of the Son of man. They did eat, they drank, they married wives, they were given in marriage, until the day that Noah entered into the ark, and the flood came, and **destroyed them all**. Likewise also as it was in the **days of Lot**; they did eat, they drank, they bought, they sold, they planted, they builded; But the same day that Lot went out of Sodom it rained fire and **BRIMSTONE** from heaven, and **destroyed them all**. *Even thus shall it be in the day when the Son of man is revealed.* (Luke 17:25-29)

And the four angels were loosed, which were prepared for an hour, and a day, and a month, and a year, for to slay the third part of men. And the number of the army of the horsemen were two hundred thousand thousand: and I heard the number of them. And thus I saw the horses in the vision, and them that sat on them, having breastplates of fire, and of jacinth, and **BRIMSTONE**: and the heads of the horses were as the heads of lions; and out of their mouths issued fire and smoke and **BRIMSTONE**. By these three was the third part of men killed, by the fire, and by the smoke, and by the **BRIMSTONE**, which issued out of their mouths. For their power is in their mouth, and in their tails: for their tails were like unto serpents, and had heads, and with them they do hurt. And the rest of the men which were not killed by these plagues **yet repented not** of the works of their hands, that they should not worship devils, and idols of gold, and silver, and brass, and stone, and of wood: which neither can see, nor hear, nor walk: **Neither repented they** of their murders, nor of their sorceries, nor of their fornication, nor of their thefts. (Revelation 9:15-21)

And I saw *another angel* fly in the midst of heaven, having the ***everlasting gospel*** to preach unto them that dwell on the earth, and to every nation, and kindred, and tongue, and people, Saying with a loud voice, *Fear God, and give glory to him*; for the hour of his ***judgment*** is come: and *worship him* that made heaven, and earth, and the sea, and the fountains of waters. And there followed *another angel,* saying, **Babylon** is fallen, is fallen, that great city, because she made all nations drink of the wine of the wrath of her **fornication**. And the *third angel* followed them, saying with a loud voice, If any man *worship* the beast and his image, and receive his *mark* in his forehead, or in his hand, The same shall drink of the wine of the **wrath of God**, which is poured out without mixture into the cup of his indignation; and he shall be tormented with fire and **BRIMSTONE** in the presence of the holy angels, and in the presence of the Lamb: And the smoke of their torment ascendeth up for ever and ever: and they have **no rest** day nor night, who worship the beast and his image, and whosoever receiveth *the mark* of his name. (Revelation 14:6-11)

And I saw **the beast**, and **the kings** of the earth, and their armies, gathered together *to make war against him that sat on the horse, and against his army.* And **the beast** was taken, and with him the **false prophet** that wrought miracles before him, with which he *deceived* them that had received the mark of the beast, and them that worshipped his image. These both were cast alive into a lake of fire burning with **BRIMSTONE**. (Revelation 19:19-20)

And they went up on the breadth of the earth, and compassed the camp of the saints about, and the beloved city: and *fire came down from God out of heaven, and devoured them.* And **the devil** that *deceived* them was cast into the lake of fire and **BRIMSTONE**, where **the beast** and **the false prophet** are, and shall be tormented day and night for ever and ever. And I saw a ***great white throne***, and him that sat on it, from whose face the earth and the heaven fled away; and there was found no place for them. And I saw the dead, small and great, stand before God; and the books were opened: and another book was opened, which is the ***book of life***: and the dead were judged out of those things which were written in the books, *according to their works*. And the sea gave up the dead which were in it; and death and hell delivered up the dead which were in them: and they were judged every man *according to their works*. And death and hell were cast into the lake of fire. This is the second death. And

whosoever was not found written in the book of life was cast into the <u>lake of fire</u>. (Revelation 20:9-15)

But the <u>fearful</u>, and <u>unbelieving</u>, and the <u>abominable</u>, and <u>murderers</u>, and <u>whoremongers</u>, and <u>sorcerers</u>, and <u>idolaters</u>, and *<u>all liars</u>,* shall have their part in the lake which burneth with fire and **BRIMSTONE: which is the second death.** (Revelation21:8)

Chapter 4

TORMENT

Therefore is the kingdom of heaven likened unto a certain *king*, which would *take account of his servants.* And when he had begun to reckon, one was brought unto him, which <u>owed him ten thousand talents</u>. But forasmuch as he had not to pay, his lord commanded him to be sold, and his wife, and children, and all that he had, and payment to be made. The servant therefore fell down, and worshipped him, saying, Lord, *have patience* with me, and I will pay thee all. Then *the lord of that servant was moved with <u>compassion</u>, and loosed him, and <u>forgave him</u> the debt.* **But** the same servant went out, and found one of his fellowservants, which owed him <u>an hundred pence</u>: and he laid hands on him, and took him by the throat, saying, Pay me that thou owest. And his fellowservant fell down at his feet, and besought him, saying, *Have patience* with me, and I will pay thee all. And **he would not**: but went and cast him into prison, till he should pay the debt. So when his fellowservants saw what was done, they were very sorry, and came and told unto their lord all that was done. Then his lord, after that he had called him, said unto him, **O thou wicked servant**, <u>I forgave thee all that debt, because thou desiredst me: Shouldest not thou also have had compassion on thy fellowservant, even as I had pity on thee</u>? And his *lord was wroth*, and delivered him to the **TORMENTORS**, till he should pay all that was due unto him. So likewise shall my heavenly Father do also unto you, if ye from your *hearts* forgive not every one his brother their trespasses. (Matthew 18:23-35)

And **in hell** he lift up his eyes, being in **TORMENTS**, and seeth Abraham afar off, and Lazarus in his bosom. And he cried and said, Father Abraham, have mercy on me, and send Lazarus, that he may dip the tip of his finger in water, and cool my tongue; for I am **TORMENTED** in this flame. But Abraham said, Son, *remember* that thou in thy lifetime receivedst thy good things, and likewise Lazarus evil things: but *now he is comforted*, *and* **thou art TORMENTED**. And beside all this, between us and you there is a great gulf fixed: so that they which would pass from hence to you cannot; neither can they pass to us, that would come from thence. Then he said, I pray thee therefore, father, that thou wouldest send him to my father's house: For I have five brethren; that he may testify unto them, lest they also come into this place of **TORMENT**. (Luke 16:23-28)

And the *fifth angel* sounded, and I saw *a star fall* from heaven unto the earth: and to him was given the **key of the bottomless pit**. And he opened the bottomless pit; and there arose a smoke out of the pit, as the smoke of a great furnace; and the sun and the air were darkened by reason of the smoke of the pit. And there came out of the smoke **locusts** upon the earth: and unto them was given power, as the <u>scorpions</u> of the earth have power. And it was commanded them that they should not hurt the grass of the earth, neither any green thing, neither any tree; but <u>only those men which have *not* the seal of God in their foreheads</u>. And to them it was given that they should not kill them, but that they should be **TORMENTED five months:** and their **TORMENT** was as the **TORMENT** of a <u>scorpion,</u> when he striketh a man. And in those days shall men seek death, and shall not find it; and shall desire to die, and death shall flee from them. And the shapes of the locusts were like unto horses prepared unto battle; and on their heads were as it were crowns like gold, and their faces were as the faces of men. And they had hair as the hair of women, and their teeth were as the teeth of lions. And they had breastplates, as it were breastplates of iron; and the sound of their wings was as the sound of chariots of many horses running to battle. And they had tails like unto scorpions, and there were stings in their tails: and <u>their power was to hurt men five months</u>. And they had **a king** over them, which is <u>the angel of the bottomless pit</u>, whose name in the Hebrew tongue is <u>Abaddon,</u> but in the Greek tongue hath his name <u>Apollyon.</u> (Revelation 9:1-11)

And there followed *another angel*, saying, **Babylon** is fallen, is fallen, that great city, because **she made *all* nations drink of the wine of the wrath of her *fornication*.** And the *third angel* followed them, saying with a loud voice, <u>If any man worship the beast and his image, and *receive his mark* in his forehead, or in his hand,</u> The same shall drink of the wine of the **wrath of God**, which is poured out without mixture into the cup of his indignation; and he shall be **TORMENTED** with fire and brimstone in the presence of the holy angels, and in the presence of the Lamb: And the smoke of their torment ascendeth up for ever and ever: and they have **no rest** day nor night, who <u>***worship the beast*** and his image, and whosoever ***receiveth the mark* of his name**</u>. (Revelation 14:8-11)

And there was given me a reed like unto a rod: and *the angel stood*, saying, Rise, and measure the temple of God, and the altar, and them that worship therein. But the court which is without the temple leave out, and measure it not; for it is given unto the Gentiles: and <u>the holy city shall they tread under foot forty and two months</u>. And I will give power unto *my two witnesses*, and they shall prophesy a thousand two hundred and threescore days, clothed in sackcloth. These are the *two olive trees*, and the *two candlesticks* standing before the God of the earth. <u>And if any man will hurt them, fire proceedeth out of their mouth, and devoureth their enemies: and if any man will hurt them, he must in this manner be killed</u>. These have power to <u>shut heaven</u>, that it <u>rain not</u> in the days of their prophecy: and have <u>power over waters</u> to turn them to <u>blood</u>, and to smite the earth with <u>all plagues</u>, as often as they will. And when they shall have finished their testimony, the <u>beast that ascendeth out of the bottomless pit shall make war against them, and shall overcome them, and kill them</u>. And their dead bodies shall lie in the street of the great city, which spiritually is called Sodom and Egypt, where also our Lord was crucified. And they of the people and kindreds and tongues and nations shall see their **dead bodies three days and an half**, and shall not suffer their dead bodies to be put in graves. And they that dwell upon the earth shall rejoice over them, and make merry, and shall send gifts one to another; because ***these two prophets* TORMENTED *them that dwelt on the earth*.** And after *three days and an half the spirit of life from God entered into them, and they stood upon their feet; and great fear fell upon them which saw them.* (Revelation 11:1-11)

And I saw *another angel* fly in the midst of heaven, having the everlasting gospel to preach unto them that dwell on the earth, and to every nation, and kindred, and tongue, and people, Saying with a loud voice, ***Fear God**, and give glory to him; for the hour of **his judgment is come:*** and worship him that made heaven, and earth, and the sea, and the fountains of waters. And there followed another angel, saying, **Babylon** is fallen, is fallen, that great city, because she made all nations drink of the wine of the wrath of her *fornication*. And the *third angel* followed them, saying with a loud voice, If any man worship the beast and his image, and *receive his mark* in his forehead, or in his hand, The same shall drink of the wine of the **wrath of God**, which is poured out without mixture into the cup of his indignation; and he shall be **TORMENTED** with fire and brimstone in the presence of the holy angels, and in the presence of the Lamb: And the smoke of their **TORMENT** ascendeth up for ever and ever: and they have *no rest* day nor night, <u>who **worship the beast** and his image, and whosoever **receiveth the mark** of his name.</u> (Revelation 14:6-11)

And after these things I saw *another angel* come down from heaven, having great power; and the earth was lightened with his glory. And he cried mightily with a strong voice, saying, **Babylon** the great is fallen, is fallen, and is become the <u>habitation of devils</u>, and the hold of <u>every foul spirit</u>, and a cage of <u>every unclean and hateful bird</u>. <u>For *all* nations have drunk of the wine of the wrath of her **fornication**, and the kings of the earth have committed **fornication** with her, and the merchants of the earth are waxed rich through the abundance of her delicacies</u>. And I heard another voice from heaven, saying, ***Come out of her, <u>my people</u>, that ye be not partakers of her sins, and that ye receive not of her plagues.*** For her **sins** have reached unto heaven, and God hath remembered her **iniquities**. Reward her even as she rewarded you, and double unto her double according to her works: in the cup which she hath filled fill to her double. How much she hath <u>glorified herself</u>, and <u>lived deliciously</u>, so much **TORMENT** and sorrow give her: for she saith in her heart, **I sit a queen**, and am no widow, and shall see no sorrow. Therefore shall <u>her plagues come in one day, death, and mourning, and famine; and she shall be utterly burned with fire</u>: *for strong is the Lord God who judgeth her.* And the kings of the earth, who have committed **fornication** and <u>lived deliciously</u> with her, shall bewail her, and lament for her, when they shall see the smoke of her burning, Standing afar off for the fear of her torment, saying, Alas, alas that great city **Babylon**, that mighty city! for **in one hour is thy judgment come.** And the merchants of the earth shall weep and mourn over her; for no man buyeth their merchandise any more: (Revelation 18:1-11)

The merchandise of gold, and silver, and precious stones, and of pearls, and fine linen, and purple, and silk, and scarlet, and all thyine wood, and all manner vessels of ivory, and all manner vessels of most precious wood, and of brass, and iron, and marble, And cinnamon, and odours, and ointments, and frankincense, and wine, and oil, and fine flour, and wheat, and beasts, and sheep, and horses, and chariots, and slaves, and souls of men. And the fruits that thy soul lusted after are departed from thee, and all things which were dainty and goodly are departed from thee, and thou shalt find them no more at all. The merchants of these things, which were made rich by her, shall stand afar off for the fear of her **TORMENT**, weeping and wailing, And saying, Alas, alas **that great city**, that was clothed in fine linen, and purple, and scarlet, and decked with gold, and precious stones, and pearls! For in one hour so great riches is come to nought. And every shipmaster, and all the company in ships, and sailors, and as many as trade by sea, stood afar off, And cried when they saw the smoke of her burning, saying, **What city is like unto this great city!** And they cast dust on their heads, and cried, weeping and wailing, saying, Alas, alas **that great city,** wherein were made rich all that had ships in the sea by reason of her costliness! for in one hour is she

TORMENT / 25

<u>made desolate</u>. *Rejoice over her, thou heaven, and ye <u>holy apostles</u> and <u>prophets</u>;* **for God hath avenged you on her.** And a mighty angel took up a stone like a great millstone, and <u>cast it into the sea</u>, saying, Thus with violence shall that **great city Babylon** be <u>thrown down</u>, and shall be found no more at all. And the voice of harpers, and musicians, and of pipers, and trumpeters, shall be heard no more at all in thee; and no craftsman, of whatsoever craft he be, shall be found any more in thee; and the sound of a millstone shall be heard no more at all in thee; And the light of a candle shall shine no more at all in thee; and the voice of the bridegroom and of the bride shall be heard no more at all in thee: for thy merchants were the great men of the earth; for **by thy sorceries were all nations deceived.** And **in her was found the blood of <u>prophets</u>, and of <u>saints</u>, and of <u>all</u> that were slain upon the earth.** (Revelation 18:12-24)

And when the thousand years are expired, **Satan** shall be loosed out of his prison, And shall go out **to deceive the nations** which are in the four quarters of the earth, <u>Gog, and Magog, to gather them together to battle</u>: the number of whom is as the sand of the sea. And they went up on the breadth of the earth, and <u>compassed the camp of the saints about, and the beloved city</u>: and *fire came down from God out of heaven, and devoured them.* And **the devil** that **deceived** them was cast into the lake of fire and brimstone, where **the beast** and **the false prophet** are, and shall be **TORMENTED** day and night for ever and ever. (Revelation 20:7-10)

Chapter 5

DARKNESS

But if thine eye be evil, thy whole body shall be full of darkness. If therefore the light that is in thee be darkness, how great is that **DARKNESS**! **No man can serve two masters:** for either he will hate the one, and love the other; or else he will hold to the one, and despise the other. **Ye *cannot* serve God and mammon.** (Matthew 6:23-24)

And when Jesus was entered into Capernaum, there came unto him **a centurion**, beseeching him, And saying, Lord, *my servant lieth at home sick of the palsy, grievously tormented.* And Jesus saith unto him, I will come and heal him. The centurion answered and said, Lord, *I am not worthy* that thou shouldest come under my roof: but *speak the word* only, and my servant shall be healed. For I am a man under authority, having soldiers under me: and I say to this man, Go, and he goeth; and to another, Come, and he cometh; and to my servant, Do this, and he doeth it. When Jesus heard it, he marvelled, and said to them that followed, Verily I say unto you, I have not found *so great faith*, no, not in Israel. And I say unto you, That many shall come from the east and west, and shall sit down with Abraham, and Isaac, and Jacob, in the kingdom of heaven. But **the children of the kingdom shall be cast out into outer DARKNESS**: there shall be

weeping and gnashing of teeth. (Matthew 8:5-12)

And Jesus answered and spake unto them again by parables, and said, The *kingdom of heaven* is like unto a certain king, which made a ***marriage for his son,*** And sent forth his servants to call them that were **bidden to the wedding**: and they would not come. Again, he sent forth other servants, saying, Tell them which are bidden, Behold, I have prepared my dinner: my oxen and my fatlings are killed, and all things are ready: come unto the marriage. But they made light of it, and went their ways, one to his farm, another to his merchandise: And the remnant took his servants, and entreated them spitefully, and slew them. But when the king heard thereof, ***he was wroth:*** and he sent forth his armies, and destroyed those murderers, *and* burned up their city. Then saith he to his servants, The wedding is ready, but **they which were bidden were not worthy**. Go ye therefore into the highways, and as many as ye shall find, bid to the marriage. So those servants went out into the highways, and gathered together all as many as they found, *both bad and good*: and the wedding was furnished with guests. And when the king came in to see the guests, he saw there a man which had not on a wedding garment: And he saith unto him, Friend, how camest thou in hither not having a ***wedding garment?*** And he was speechless. Then said the king to the servants, Bind him hand and foot, and take him away, and cast him into outer **DARKNESS**, there shall be weeping and gnashing of teeth. (Matthew 22:1-13)

Then he which had received the **one talent** came and said, Lord, I knew thee that ***thou art an hard man***, *reaping where thou hast not sown, and gathering where thou hast not strawed*: And I was afraid, and went and hid thy talent in the earth: lo, there thou hast that is thine. His lord answered and said unto him, Thou **wicked and slothful servant**, thou knewest that *I reap where I sowed not*, and *gather where I have not strawed*: Thou oughtest therefore to have put my money to the exchangers, and then at my coming I should have received mine own with usury. Take therefore the talent from him, and give it unto him which hath ten talents. For unto every one that hath shall be given, and he shall have abundance: but from him that hath not shall be taken away even that which he hath. And **cast ye the unprofitable servant into outer DARKNESS**: there shall be weeping and gnashing of teeth. (Matthew 25:24-30)

The light of the body is the eye: therefore when thine *eye is single*, thy whole body also is full of light; but when thine eye is evil, thy body also is full of **DARKNESS**. **Take heed** therefore that the light which is in thee be not **DARKNESS**. If thy whole body therefore be full of light, having *no* part **DARK**, the whole shall be full of light, as when the bright shining of a candle doth give thee light. (Luke 11:34-36)

And the light shineth in **DARKNESS**; and **the DARKNESS comprehended it not.** (John 1:5)

And this is the condemnation, that light is come into the world, and **men loved DARKNESS rather than light**, *because* their deeds were evil. For every one that doeth evil hateth the light, neither cometh to the light, lest his deeds should be reproved. (John 3:19-20)

Then Jesus said unto them, Yet a little while is the light with you. Walk while ye have the light, lest darkness come upon you: for **he that walketh in DARKNESS knoweth** *not* **whither he goeth**. (John 12:35)

For the *wrath of God* is revealed from heaven against *all* ungodliness and unrighteousness of men, who hold the truth in unrighteousness; Because that which may be known of God is manifest in them; for God hath shewed it unto them. For the invisible things of him from the creation of the world are *clearly seen*, being understood by the things that are made, even his eternal power and Godhead; so that they are *without excuse*: Because that, when they knew God, they glorified him not as God, neither were thankful; but became **vain in their imaginations,** *and* **their foolish heart** was **DARKENED**. (Romans 1:18-21)

This I say therefore, and testify in the Lord, that ye henceforth **walk** *not* **as other Gentiles walk**, in the vanity of their mind, Having the understanding **DARKENED**, being alienated from the life of God through the ignorance that is in them, because of the blindness of their heart: Who being **past feeling have given themselves over** unto lasciviousness, to work <u>all uncleanness</u> with <u>greediness</u>. (Ephesians 4:17-19)

But <u>fornication</u>, and ***all*** <u>uncleanness</u>, or <u>covetousness</u>, let it not be once named among you, as becometh saints; Neither <u>filthiness</u>, nor <u>foolish talking</u>, nor <u>jesting</u>, which are not convenient: but *rather giving of thanks*. For this ye know, that no <u>whoremonger</u>, nor <u>unclean</u> person, nor <u>covetous</u> man, who is an <u>idolater</u>, hath *any* inheritance in the kingdom of Christ and of God. Let no man deceive you with vain words: for because of these things cometh the **wrath of God** upon <u>the children of disobedience</u>. Be not ye therefore partakers with them. For ye were sometimes **DARKNESS**, but ***now*** are ye light in the Lord: walk as children of light: And **have *no* <u>fellowship with the unfruitful works of</u> DARKNESS**, but *rather **reprove** them*. For it is a <u>shame</u> even to speak of those things which are done of them in secret. (Ephesians 5:3-8, 11-12)

Put on the whole armour of God, that ye may be able to stand against the wiles of the devil. For we wrestle not against flesh and blood, but against <u>principalities</u>, against <u>powers</u>, against the <u>rulers of the **DARKNESS** of *this* world</u>, against <u>spiritual wickedness in high places</u>. Wherefore take unto you ***the whole armour of God***, that ye may be able to ***withstand*** in the evil day, and having done all, to ***stand***. (Ephesians 6:11-13)

But there were **false prophets** also among the people, even as there shall be **false teachers** among you, who privily shall bring in **damnable heresies**, even denying the Lord that bought them, and bring upon themselves swift destruction. And *many* shall follow their pernicious ways; by reason of whom the way of truth shall be evil spoken of. And through covetousness shall they with feigned words make merchandise of you: whose judgment now of a long time lingereth not, and their damnation slumbereth not. For if *God spared not* the angels that sinned, but cast them down to hell, and delivered them into chains of **DARKNESS**, to be reserved unto judgment; And *spared not* the old world, but *saved Noah* the eighth person, a preacher of righteousness, bringing in *the flood* upon the world of the ungodly; And turning the cities of Sodom and Gomorrha into ashes condemned them with an overthrow, making them <u>**an ensample** unto those that after should live ungodly</u>; And delivered just Lot, vexed with the filthy conversation of the wicked: (For that righteous man dwelling among them, in seeing and hearing, vexed his righteous soul from day to day with <u>their unlawful deeds</u>;) *The Lord knoweth how to deliver the godly out of temptations*, and <u>**to reserve the unjust unto the day of judgment to be punished**</u>: (2 Peter 2:1-9)

But these, as **natural brute beasts**, made to be taken and destroyed, speak evil of the things that they understand not; and <u>**shall utterly perish** in their own corruption</u>; And <u>shall receive the reward of *un*righteousness</u>, as they that count it pleasure to riot in the day time. <u>Spots</u> they are and <u>blemishes</u>, sporting themselves with **their own deceivings** while they feast with you; Having eyes full of adultery, and that **cannot cease from sin**; beguiling unstable souls: an heart they have exercised with covetous practices; *cursed* children: Which have **forsaken the right way**, and are gone astray, following the way of Balaam the son of Bosor, who *loved* the wages of unrighteousness; But was rebuked for his iniquity: the dumb ass speaking with man's voice forbad the madness of the prophet. These are wells without water, clouds that are carried with a tempest; to whom the mist of **DARKNESS** is reserved for ever. For when they speak great swelling words of vanity, they allure through the lusts of the flesh, through much wantonness, those that were clean escaped from them who live in error. While they promise them liberty, they themselves are the **servants of corruption:** for of whom a man is overcome, of the same is he brought in bondage. (2Peter 2:12-19)

If we say that we have fellowship with him (God), and **walk (live) in DARKNESS** (sin), **we lie**, and do not the truth: (1 John 1:6)

He that saith he is in the light, and hateth his brother, is in **DARKNESS** even until now. But he that hateth his brother is in **DARKNESS**, and **walketh in DARKNESS**, and knoweth not whither he goeth, because that **DARKNESS** hath blinded his eyes. (1 John 2:9,11)

And the angels which kept not their first estate, but left their own habitation, he hath reserved in everlasting chains under **DARKNESS** unto the **judgment** of the great day. Even as Sodom and

Gomorrha, and the cities about them in like manner, giving themselves over to <u>fornication</u>, and going after <u>strange flesh</u>, are **set forth for <u>an example</u>**, suffering the vengeance of eternal fire. (Jude 1:6-7)

But these speak evil of those things which they know not: but what they know naturally, as <u>brute beasts,</u> in those things **they corrupt themselves.** Woe unto them! for they have gone in the way of Cain, and ran greedily after the error of Balaam for reward, and perished in the gainsaying of Core. These are spots in your feasts of charity, when they feast with you, feeding themselves <u>without fear: clouds they are without water,</u> <u>carried about of winds</u>; trees whose <u>fruit withereth,</u> <u>without fruit, twice dead, plucked up by the roots;</u> <u>Raging waves of the sea,</u> **foaming out their own shame**; <u>wandering stars,</u> to whom is reserved the blackness of **DARKNESS** for ever. (Jude 1:10-13)

And the *fourth angel* sounded, and the third part of the sun was smitten, and the third part of the moon, and the third part of the stars; so as the third part of them was **DARKENED**, and the day shone not for a third part of it, and the night likewise. And I beheld, and heard an angel flying through the midst of heaven, saying with a loud voice, **Woe, woe, woe, to the inhabiters of the earth** by reason of the other voices of the trumpet of the three angels, which are yet to sound! (Revelation 8:12-13)

And the *fifth angel* sounded, and I saw a star fall from heaven unto the earth: and to him was given the key of the bottomless pit. And he opened the bottomless pit; and there arose a smoke out of the pit, as the smoke of a great furnace; and the sun and the air were **DARKENED** by reason of the smoke of the pit. And there came out of the smoke **locusts** upon the earth: and unto them was given power, as the scorpions of the earth have power. And it was commanded them that they should not hurt the grass of the earth, neither any green thing, neither any tree; but **only those men which have *not* the seal of God in their foreheads.** And to them it was given that they should not kill them, but that they should be **tormented five months**: and their torment was as the torment of a scorpion, when he striketh a man. And in those days shall men seek death, and shall not find it; and shall desire to die, and death shall flee from them. (Revelation 9:1-6)

And the *fourth angel* poured out his vial upon the sun; and power was given unto him **to scorch men** with fire. And men were scorched with great heat, and blasphemed the name of God, which hath power over these plagues: and **they repented not** to give him glory. And the *fifth angel* poured out his vial upon **the seat of the beast**; and his kingdom was full of **DARKNESS**; and they gnawed their tongues for pain, And blasphemed the God of heaven because of their pains and their sores, and **repented not of their deeds.** (Revelation 16:8-11)

Chapter 6

LAKE OF FIRE

And I saw **the beast**, and **the kings** of the earth, and **their armies**, gathered together to make war against *him that sat on the horse, and against his army.* And the beast was taken, and with him the false prophet that wrought miracles before him, with which he **deceived** them that had received the mark of the beast, *and* them that worshipped his image. These both were cast alive into a **LAKE OF FIRE** burning with brimstone. (Revelation 19:19-20)

And when the thousand years are expired, **Satan** shall be loosed out of his prison, And shall go out **to** *deceive* **the nations** which are in the four quarters of the earth, Gog, and Magog, to gather them together to battle: the number of whom is as the sand of the sea. And they went up on the breadth of the earth, and compassed the camp of the saints about, and the beloved city: and *fire came down from God out of heaven, and devoured them.* And **the devil that** *deceived* **them** was cast into the **LAKE OF FIRE** and brimstone, where the beast and the false prophet are, and shall be tormented day and night for ever and ever. And I saw a ***great white throne***, and him that sat on it, from whose face the earth and the heaven fled away; and there was found no place for them. And I saw the dead, small and great, ***stand before God;*** and the books were opened: and another book was opened, which is *the book of life*: and the dead were **judged** out of those things which were written in the books, *according to their works*. And the sea gave up the dead which were in it; and death and hell delivered up the dead which were in them: and they were **judged** *every man according to their works*. And death and hell were cast into the **LAKE OF FIRE**. This is the second death. And **whosoever was *not* found written in the book of life was cast into the LAKE OF FIRE.** (Revelation 20:7-15)

Chapter 7

INDIGNATION

Therefore **thou art *in*excusable, O man,** whosoever thou art that judgest: for wherein thou judgest another, thou condemnest thyself; <u>for thou that judgest doest the same things</u>. But we are sure that the judgment of God is according to truth against them which commit such things. And thinkest thou this, O man, that <u>judgest them which do such things, and doest the same</u>, that thou shalt escape the judgment of God? Or ***<u>despisest</u>*** *thou the riches of his goodness and forbearance and longsuffering;* <u>not knowing</u> *that the goodness of God leadeth thee to* **repentance?** But after <u>thy hardness and impenitent heart treasurest</u> up unto thyself **wrath** against the day of wrath and revelation of the righteous judgment of God; Who will render to every man *according to his deeds*: To them who by *patient continuance in well doing seek for glory and honour and immortality,* **eternal life***:* But unto them that are <u>contentious</u>, and <u>do ***not*** obey the truth</u>, but <u>obey **un**righteousness</u>, **INDIGNATION** and **wrath, Tribulation** and **anguish**, upon every soul of man that <u>doeth evil,</u> of the Jew first, and also of the Gentile; (Romans 2:1-9)

For if we **sin wilfully** *after* that we have received the knowledge of the truth, <u>there remaineth no more sacrifice for sins</u>, But a certain fearful looking for of judgment and fiery **INDIGNATION**, which shall devour the adversaries. He that **despised** Moses' law **died** without mercy under two or three witnesses: Of how much **sorer punishment**, suppose ye, shall he be thought worthy, who hath **trodden under foot the Son of God,** and hath counted the blood of the covenant, wherewith he was sanctified, an unholy thing, and hath done despite unto the Spirit of grace? For we know him that hath said, *Vengeance belongeth unto me, I will recompense, saith the Lord.* And again, The Lord shall judge *his* people. *It is a fearful thing to fall into the hands of the living God.* (Hebrews 10:26-31)

And the *third angel* followed them, saying with a loud voice, If any man **worship the beast** and his image, *and* receive **his mark** in his forehead, or in his hand, The same shall drink of the wine of the *wrath of God*, which is poured out without mixture into the cup of his **INDIGNATION**; and he shall be tormented with fire and brimstone in the presence of the holy angels, and in the presence of the Lamb: And the smoke of their torment ascendeth up for ever and ever: and they have **no rest** day nor night, who **worship the beast** and his image, *and* whosoever receiveth **the mark** of his name. (Revelation 14:9-11)

Chapter 8

EVERLASTING

But <u>whoso shall **offend** one of these little ones which believe in me</u>, it were better for him that a millstone were hanged about his neck, and that he were drowned in the depth of the sea. **Woe** unto the world because of offences! for it must needs be that offences come; but **woe** to that man by whom the offence cometh! Wherefore <u>if thy **hand** or thy **foot** offend thee</u>, *cut them off*, and cast them from thee: it is better for thee to enter into life halt or maimed, rather than having two hands or two feet to be cast into **EVERLASTING** fire. And <u>if thine **eye** offend thee</u>, *pluck it out*, and cast it from thee: it is better for thee to enter into life with one eye, rather than having two eyes to be **cast into hell fire**. (Matthew 18:6-9)

Then shall he say also unto them on the **left hand**, Depart from me, **ye cursed**, into **EVERLASTING** fire, prepared for the devil and his angels: For I was an *hungred*, and <u>ye gave me no meat</u>: I was *thirsty*, and <u>ye gave me no drink</u>: I was *a stranger*, and ye <u>took me not in</u>: *naked*, and <u>ye clothed me not</u>: *sick*, and *in prison*, and <u>ye visited me not</u>. Then shall they also answer him, saying, Lord, when saw we thee an hungred, or athirst, or a stranger, or naked, or sick, or in prison, and did not minister unto thee? Then shall he answer them, saying, Verily I say unto you, **Inasmuch as ye did it *not* to one of the least of these, ye did it *not* to me.** And these shall go away into **EVERLASTING** punishment: but the *righteous into life eternal.* (Matthew 25:41-46)

Seeing it is a righteous thing with God to recompense tribulation to them that trouble you; And to you who are troubled rest with us, when the *Lord Jesus* shall be revealed from heaven with his mighty angels, In flaming fire *taking vengeance on them* that know not God, and that obey not the gospel of our Lord Jesus Christ: Who shall be **punished with EVERLASTING destruction** *from the presence of the Lord,* and *from the glory of his power;* (2 Thessalonians 1:6-9)

And the angels which kept not their first estate, but left their own habitation, he hath reserved in **EVERLASTING** chains under darkness unto the *judgment of the great day.* Even as Sodom and Gomorrha, and the cities about them in like manner, giving themselves over to fornication, and going after strange flesh, are **set forth for an example, suffering the vengeance of eternal fire.** (Jude 1:6-7)

Chapter 9

CONDEMN

O generation of vipers, how can ye, being evil, speak good things? for **out of the abundance of the heart the mouth speaketh**. A *good man* out of the good treasure of the heart bringeth forth *good things:* and an <u>evil man</u> out of the <u>evil treasure</u> bringeth forth <u>evil things</u>. But I say unto you, That ***every idle word*** *that men shall speak, they shall give account thereof in the day of judgment.* For by thy *words* thou shalt be *<u>justified</u>*, and by thy <u>words</u> thou shalt be **CONDEMNED**. (Matthew 12:34-37)

Then certain of the scribes and of the Pharisees answered, saying, Master, we would see a sign from thee. But he answered and said unto them, <u>An evil and adulterous generation seeketh after a sign</u>; and there shall no sign be given to it, but the sign of the prophet Jonas: For as Jonas was three days and three nights in the whale's belly; *so shall the Son of man be three days and three nights in the heart of the earth.* The men of Nineveh shall rise in judgment with this generation, and shall **CONDEMN** it: because ***they repented*** at the preaching of Jonas; and, behold, a greater than Jonas is here. The queen of the south shall rise up in the judgment with this generation, and shall **CONDEMN** it: for she came from the uttermost parts of the earth to hear the wisdom of Solomon; and, behold, *a greater than Solomon is here.* (Matthew 12:38-42)

And when the people were gathered thick together, he began to say, This is an evil generation: they seek a sign; and there shall no sign be given it, but the sign of Jonas the prophet. *For as Jonas was a sign unto the Ninevites, so shall also the Son of man be to this generation.* The queen of the south shall rise up in the judgment with the men of this generation, and **CONDEMN** them: for she came from the utmost parts of the earth to hear the wisdom of Solomon; and, behold, *a greater than Solomon is here.* The men of Nineve shall rise up in the judgment with this generation, and shall **CONDEMN** it: for *they repented* at the preaching of Jonas; and, *behold, a greater than Jonas is here.* (Luke 11:29-32)

And one of the malefactors which were hanged railed on him, saying, If thou be Christ, save thyself and us. But the other answering rebuked him, saying, *Dost not thou fear God,* seeing thou art in the same **CONDEMNATION?** And we indeed justly; for we receive the due reward of our deeds: but this man hath done nothing amiss. (Luke 23:39-41)

He that *believeth* on him is *not* **CONDEMNED**: but he that believeth not *is* **CONDEMNED** *already*, because he hath not believed in the name of the only begotten Son of God. And this is the

CONDEMNATION, that light is come into the world, and **men loved darkness rather than light, because their deeds were evil.** For every one that doeth evil <u>hateth the light</u>, neither cometh to the light, lest his deeds should be reproved. (John 3:18-20)

Therefore **thou art inexcusable, O man,** whosoever thou art that judgest: for wherein thou judgest another, thou **CONDEMNEST** thyself; for thou that judgest <u>doest the same things</u>. But we are sure that the judgment of God is according to truth against them which commit such things. And thinkest thou this, O man, <u>that judgest them which do such things, and doest the same</u>, that thou shalt escape the *judgment of God?* (Romans 2:1-3)

And not as it was <u>by *one* that sinned</u>, so is the gift: for the judgment was by *one* to **CONDEMNATION**, but the free gift is of many offences unto justification. Therefore as by the <u>offence of *one*</u> **judgment came upon all men to CONDEMNATION**; even so *by the righteousness of one* the free gift came upon all men unto justification of life. (Romans 5:16,18)

For I have received of the Lord that which also I delivered unto you, that the Lord Jesus the same night in which he was betrayed took bread: And when he had given thanks, he brake it, and said, Take, eat: this is my body, which is broken for you: this do in remembrance of me. After the same manner also he took the cup, when he had supped, saying, this cup is the new testament in my blood: this do ye, as oft as ye drink it, in remembrance of me. For as often as ye eat this bread, and drink this cup, ye do shew the Lord's death till he come. *Wherefore* whosoever shall eat this bread, and drink this cup of the Lord, **unworthily**, shall be **guilty of the body and blood of the Lord.** But *let a man examine himself,* and so let him eat of that bread, and drink of that cup. For he that eateth and drinketh **unworthily, eateth and drinketh damnation to himself,** not discerning the Lord's body. For this cause many are weak and sickly among you, and many sleep. For if we would *judge ourselves*, we should not be judged. But when we are judged, we are *chastened of the Lord*, that we should not be **CONDEMNED** with the world. Wherefore, my brethren, when ye come together to eat, tarry one for another. And if any man hunger, let him eat at home; that ye come not together unto **CONDEMNATION**. And the rest will I set in order when I come. (1 Corinthians 11:23-34)

A man that is an heretick **after the first and second admonition reject;** Knowing that he that is such is subverted, and sinneth, being **CONDEMNED** of himself. (Titus 3: 10-11)

My brethren, be not many masters, knowing that we shall receive the greater **CONDEMNATION**. For in *many* things we offend all. If any man offend not in word, the same is a perfect man, and able also to bridle the whole body. Behold, we put bits in the horses' mouths, that they may obey us; and we turn about their whole body. Behold also the ships, which though they be so great, and are driven of fierce winds, yet are they turned about with a very small helm, whithersoever the governor listeth. Even so **the tongue** is a little member, and boasteth great things. Behold, how great a matter a little fire kindleth! And **the tongue is a fire, a world of iniquity:** so is the tongue among our members, that it defileth the whole body, and setteth on fire the course of nature; and it is set on fire of hell. (James 3:1-6)

Go to now, **ye rich men, weep and howl for your miseries that shall come upon you.** Your riches are corrupted, and your garments are *motheaten*. Your gold and silver is cankered; and the rust of them *shall be a witness against you, and shall eat your flesh as it were fire.* Ye have heaped treasure together for the last days. Behold, the hire of the labourers who have reaped down your fields, which is of you kept back by fraud, crieth: and the cries of them which have reaped are entered into the ears of the Lord of sabaoth. Ye have lived in pleasure on the earth, and been wanton; ye have nourished your hearts, as in a day of slaughter. Ye have **CONDEMNED** and killed the just; and he doth not resist you.(James5:1-6)

Grudge not one against another, brethren, lest ye be **CONDEMNED**: behold, the judge standeth before the door. Take, my brethren, *the prophets*, who have spoken in the name of the Lord, for an example of *suffering affliction, and of patience.* **Behold, we** *count them happy which endure*. Ye have heard of the patience of Job, and have seen the end of the Lord; that the Lord is very pitiful, and of tender mercy. But above all things, my brethren, <u>swear **not**</u>, neither by heaven, neither by the earth, neither by any other oath: but let your yea be yea; and your nay, nay; lest ye fall into **CONDEMNATION**. (James 5:9-12)

But there were **false prophets** also among the people, even as there shall be **false teachers** among you, who privily shall bring in **<u>damnable heresies,</u>** even <u>denying the Lord</u> that bought them, and bring upon themselves swift destruction. And <u>*many* shall follow their pernicious ways</u>; by reason of whom the way of truth shall be evil spoken of. And through covetousness shall they with feigned words make merchandise of you: whose judgment now of a long time lingereth not, and <u>their damnation slumbereth not</u>. For *if God spared not the angels that sinned,* but cast them down to hell, and delivered them into chains of darkness, to be reserved unto *judgment;* And <u>spared not the old world</u>, but saved *Noah* the eighth person, a preacher of righteousness, bringing in the flood upon the world of <u>the ungodly</u>; And turning the cities of Sodom and Gomorrha into ashes **CONDEMNED** them with an overthrow, **making them an ensample** <u>unto those that after should</u> **live ungodly**; And delivered just Lot, *vexed* with the <u>filthy conversation of the wicked</u>: (For that righteous man dwelling among them, in seeing and hearing, *vexed* his righteous soul from day to day with their <u>unlawful deeds</u>;) The Lord knoweth how to deliver the godly out of temptations, and **to reserve the unjust unto the day of judgment to be punished**: (2 Peter 2:1-9)

Beloved, when I gave all diligence to write unto you of the common salvation, it was needful for me to write unto you, and exhort you that ye should *earnestly contend for the faith* which was once delivered unto the saints. For there are certain men crept in unawares, who were before of old ordained to this **CONDEMNATION**, ungodly men, turning the grace of our God into lasciviousness, and denying the only Lord God, and our Lord Jesus Christ. (Jude 1:3-4)

Chapter 10

CORRUPTION

Lay *not* up for yourselves treasures upon earth, where moth and rust doth **CORRUPT**, and where thieves break through and steal: But *lay up for yourselves treasures in heaven*, where neither moth nor rust doth **CORRUPT**, and where thieves do not break through nor steal: *For where your treasure is, there will your heart be also.* (Matthew 6:19-21)

Beware of false prophets, which come to you in sheep's clothing, but inwardly they are ravening wolves. **Ye shall know them by their fruits.** Do men gather grapes of thorns, or figs of thistles? Even so every *good tree* bringeth forth *good fruit*; but a **CORRUPT** tree bringeth forth evil fruit. A good tree cannot bring forth evil fruit, neither can a **CORRUPT** tree bring forth good fruit. *Every tree that bringeth not forth good fruit is hewn down, and cast into the fire.* Wherefore by their fruits ye shall know them. (Matthew 7:15-20)

Be not deceived: evil communications **CORRUPT** good manners. (1 Corinthians 15:33)

Now this I say, brethren, **that flesh and blood cannot inherit the kingdom of God**; neither doth

CORRUPTION inherit incorruption. (1 Corinthians 15:50)

For we are not as *many*, which **CORRUPT the word of God:** but as of sincerity, but as of God, in the sight of God speak we in Christ. (2 Corinthians 2:17)

Be not deceived; God is not mocked: for whatsoever a man soweth, that shall he also reap. For he that soweth to his flesh shall of the flesh reap **CORRUPTION**; *but* he that soweth to the Spirit shall of the *Spirit reap life everlasting.* (Galatians 6:7-8)

If so be that ye have heard him, and have been taught by him, as the truth is in Jesus: That **ye *put off* concerning the former conversation the old man,** which is **CORRUPT** according to the deceitful lusts; (Ephesians 4:21-22)

Let *no* **CORRUPT communication** proceed out of your mouth, *but* that which is *good* to the use of edifying, that it may minister grace unto the hearers. (Ephesians 4:29)

If any man teach otherwise, and consent not to wholesome words, even the words of our Lord Jesus Christ, and to the doctrine which is according to godliness; He is proud, knowing nothing, but doting about questions and strifes of words, whereof cometh envy, strife, railings, evil surmisings,

CORRUPTION / 50

Perverse disputings of men of **CORRUPT** minds, and destitute of the truth, supposing that gain is godliness: *from such withdraw thyself.* (1 Timothy 6:3-5)

This know also, that **in the last days** *perilous times shall come.* For men shall be lovers of their own selves, covetous, boasters, proud, blasphemers, disobedient to parents, unthankful, unholy, Without natural affection, trucebreakers, false accusers, incontinent, fierce, despisers of those that are good, Traitors, heady, highminded, lovers of pleasures more than lovers of God; Having a form of godliness, but denying the power thereof: *from such turn away.* For of this sort are they which creep into houses, and lead captive silly women laden with sins, led away with divers lusts, Ever learning, and never able to come to the knowledge of the truth. Now as Jannes and Jambres withstood Moses, so do these also resist the truth: men of **CORRUPT** minds, reprobate concerning the faith. But they shall proceed no further: for their folly shall be manifest unto all men, as their's also was. (2 Timothy 3:1-9)

Go to now, **ye rich men**, weep and howl for your miseries that shall come upon you. Your riches are **CORRUPTED**, and your garments are motheaten. Your gold and silver is cankered; and the rust of them shall be a witness against you, and shall eat your flesh as it were fire. Ye have heaped treasure together for the last days. Behold, the hire of the labourers who have reaped down your fields, which is of you kept back by fraud, crieth: and the cries of them which have reaped are entered into the ears of the Lord of sabaoth. Ye have <u>lived in pleasure</u> on the earth, and <u>been wanton;</u> ye have <u>nourished your hearts,</u> as in a day of slaughter. Ye have <u>condemned</u> and <u>killed the just</u>; and he doth not resist you. (James 5:1-6)

Whereby are given unto us exceeding great and precious promises: that ***by these ye might be partakers of the divine nature***, having *escaped* the **CORRUPTION** that is in the world through <u>lust</u>. (2 Peter 1:4)

But these, as natural **brute beasts**, made to be taken and destroyed, speak evil of the things that they understand not; and **shall utterly perish in their own CORRUPTION**; And shall receive the reward of <u>unrighteousness</u>, as they that count it <u>pleasure to riot in the day time</u>. Spots they are and blemishes, sporting themselves with **their own deceivings** while they feast with you; Having eyes full of <u>adultery</u>, and that **cannot cease from sin**; beguiling unstable souls: an heart they have exercised with <u>covetous practices</u>; **cursed children:** Which have **forsaken the right way**, and are gone astray, following the way of Balaam the son of Bosor, who *loved* the wages of *un*righteousness; (2 Peter 2:12-15)

These are <u>wells without water</u>, clouds that are <u>carried with a tempest</u>; to whom the mist of darkness is reserved for ever. For when they <u>speak great swelling words of vanity</u>, they allure through the lusts of the flesh, through much wantonness, those that were clean escaped from them who live in error. While they promise them liberty, they themselves are the **SERVANTS OF CORRUPTION**: for of whom a man is overcome, of the same is he brought in bondage. For *if after they have escaped the pollutions of the world through the knowledge of the Lord and Saviour Jesus Christ,* **they are again entangled therein, and overcome, the latter end is worse with them than the beginning.** *For it had been better for them not to have known the way of righteousness, than, after they have known it, to turn from the holy commandment delivered unto them.* But it is happened unto them according to the true proverb, The dog is turned to his own vomit again; *and* the sow that was washed to her wallowing in the mire. (2 Peter 2:17-22)

But these speak evil of those things which they know not: but what they know naturally, as brute beasts, in those things **they CORRUPT themselves**. (Jude 1:10)

For true and righteous are his judgments: for he hath judged **the great whore**, which did **CORRUPT the earth with her fornication,** and *hath avenged the blood of his servants at her hand.* (Revelation 19:2)

Chapter 11

DESTROY

And fear not them which kill the body, but are not able to kill the soul: but rather *fear him which is able to* **DESTROY** *both soul and body in hell.* (Matthew 10:28)

When the lord therefore of the vineyard cometh, <u>what will he do</u> unto those husbandmen? They say unto him, **He will miserably DESTROY those wicked men**, and will *let out his vineyard unto other husbandmen, which shall render him the fruits in their seasons.* (Matthew 21:40-41)

And Jesus answered and spake unto them again by parables, and said, *The kingdom of heaven is like unto a certain king, which <u>made a marriage for his son,</u>* And sent forth his servants to call them that were bidden to the wedding: and **they would not come**. Again, he sent forth other servants, saying, Tell them which are bidden, Behold, I have prepared my dinner: my oxen and my fatlings are killed, and all things are ready: come unto the marriage. But **they made light of it**, and went their ways, one to his farm, another to his merchandise: And the remnant took his servants, and entreated them spitefully, and slew them. But when the king heard thereof, *he was wroth:* and he sent forth his armies, and **DESTROYED** those murderers, and burned up their city. Then saith he to his servants, The wedding is ready, but they which were bidden were **not worthy**. (Matthew 22:1-8)

And he began to speak unto them by parables. **A certain man planted a vineyard**, and set an hedge about it, and digged a place for the winefat, and built a tower, and let it out to husbandmen, and went into a far country. And at the season he sent to the husbandmen *a servant*, that he might receive from the husbandmen of the fruit of the vineyard. And they caught him, and <u>beat him</u>, and sent him away empty. And again he sent unto them *another servant*; and at him <u>they cast stones</u>, and <u>wounded him in the head</u>, and sent him away <u>shamefully handled</u>. And again he sent *another;* and him <u>they killed</u>, and many others; <u>beating</u> some, and <u>killing</u> some.   Having yet therefore *one son,* his wellbeloved, he sent him also last unto them, saying, They will reverence my son. But those husbandmen said among themselves, This is the heir; come, let us kill him, and the inheritance shall be ours. <u>And they took him, and killed him, and cast him out of the vineyard</u>. *What shall therefore the lord of the vineyard do?* **he will come and DESTROY the husbandmen,** *and* **will give the vineyard unto others.** And have ye not read this scripture; The stone which the builders rejected is become the head of the corner: (Mark 12:1-10)

And as it was in the days of Noe, so shall it be also in the days of the Son of man. They did eat, they drank, they married wives, they were given in marriage, until the day that Noah entered into the ark, and **the flood came, and DESTROYED them all.** Likewise also <u>as it was in the days of Lot</u>; they did eat, they drank, they bought, they sold, they planted, they builded; But the same day that Lot went out of Sodom **it rained fire and brimstone from heaven, and DESTROYED them all.** Even thus shall it be in the day when the Son of man is revealed. (Luke 17:26-30)

Then began he to speak to the people this parable; <u>A certain man planted a vineyard, and let it forth to husbandmen</u>, and went into a far country for a long time. And at the season *he sent a servant* to the husbandmen, that they should give him of the fruit of the vineyard: but <u>the husbandmen beat him</u>, and sent him away empty. And again he sent *another servant*: and <u>they beat him also</u>, and <u>entreated him shamefully</u>, and sent him away empty. And again he sent *a third*: and <u>they wounded him</u> also, and cast him out. Then said the lord of the vineyard, *What shall I do?* I will send my beloved son: it may be they will reverence him when they see him. But when the husbandmen saw him, they reasoned among themselves, saying, This is the heir: <u>come, let us kill him, that the inheritance may be ours</u>. So they cast him out of the vineyard, and killed him. *What therefore shall the lord of the vineyard do unto them?* **He shall come and DESTROY these husbandmen,** and shall give the vineyard to others. And when they heard it, they said, **God forbid.** And he beheld them, and said, What is this then that is written, The stone which the builders rejected, the same is become the head of the corner? (Luke 20:9-17)

The thief cometh not, but for to **<u>steal</u>**, and to **<u>kill</u>**, and to **<u>DESTROY</u>**: I am come that they might have *life*, and that they might have it more abundantly. (John 10:10)

And he shall send Jesus Christ, which before was preached unto you: Whom the heaven must receive until the times of restitution of all things, which God hath spoken by the mouth of all his holy prophets since the world began. For Moses truly said unto the fathers, *A prophet* shall the Lord your God raise up unto you of your brethren, like unto me; *him shall ye hear in all things whatsoever he shall say unto you.* And it shall come to pass, that **every soul, which will *not* hear that prophet, shall be DESTROYED** from among the people. (Acts 3:20-23)

Knowing this, that *our old man is **crucified*** with him, that the body of sin might be **DESTROYED**, that henceforth **we should not serve sin.** (Romans 6:6)

For it is written, I will **DESTROY** the wisdom of the wise, and will bring to nothing the understanding of the prudent. Where is the wise? where is the scribe? where is the disputer of this world? hath not God made foolish the wisdom of this world? For after that in the wisdom of God **the world by wisdom knew not God,** it pleased God by the foolishness of preaching to *save them that believe.* (1 Corinthians 1:19-21)

If any man defile the temple of God, **him shall God**

DESTROY; for the temple of God is holy, *which temple ye are*. (1 Corinthians 3:17)

But **with many of them God was not well pleased:** for they were overthrown in the wilderness. Now these things were **our examples**, to the intent *we should not lust after evil things*, as they also lusted. Neither be ye idolaters, as were some of them; as it is written, The people sat down to eat and drink, and rose up to play. Neither let us commit fornication, as some of them committed, and fell in one day three and twenty thousand. Neither let us tempt Christ, as some of them also tempted, and were **DESTROYED** of serpents. Neither murmur ye, as some of them also murmured, and were **DESTROYED** of the destroyer. *Now all these things happened unto them for examples: and they are written for our admonition,* upon whom the ends of the world are come. Wherefore let him that thinketh he standeth *take heed* lest he fall. (1 Corinthians 10:5-12)

Then cometh **the end,** when he shall have delivered up the kingdom to God, even the Father; when he shall have put down all rule and all authority and power. For *he must reign, till he hath put all enemies under his feet.* The last enemy that shall be **DESTROYED** is death. (1 Corinthians 15:24-26)

Let no man deceive you by any means: for that day shall not come, except there come a falling away first, and that **man of sin** be revealed, the **son of perdition; Who opposeth and exalteth himself above all that is called God**, or that is worshipped;

so that **he as God sitteth in the temple of God, shewing himself that he is God.** Remember ye not, that, when I was yet with you, I told you these things? And now ye know what withholdeth that he might be revealed in his time. For the mystery of iniquity doth already work: only he who now letteth will let, until he be taken out of the way. And then shall that Wicked be revealed, *whom the Lord shall consume* with the spirit of his mouth, *and shall* **DESTROY** *with the brightness of his coming:* (2 Thessalonians 2:3-8)

Speak not evil one of another, *brethren.* He that speaketh evil of his brother, and judgeth his brother, speaketh evil of the law, and judgeth the law: but if thou judge the law, thou art not a doer of the law, but a judge. *There is one lawgiver, who is able to save and to* **DESTROY**: who art thou that judgest another? (James 4:11-12)

He that committeth sin is of the devil; for the devil sinneth from the beginning. For this purpose the Son of God was manifested, that he might **DESTROY** the works of the devil. (1 John 3:8)

For there are certain men crept in *unawares*, who were before of old ordained to this condemnation, **ungodly men, turning the grace of our God into lasciviousness,** *and* denying the only Lord God, and our Lord Jesus Christ. I will therefore put you in remembrance, though ye once knew this, how that the Lord, having saved the people out of the land of

Egypt, afterward **DESTROYED** them that believed not. (Jude 1:4-5)

And the nations were angry, and *thy wrath is come,* and the time of the dead, that they should be **judged,** and that thou shouldest give *reward* unto *thy servants the prophets*, and *to the saints*, and *them that fear thy name*, small and great; and shouldest **DESTROY** **them which destroy the earth.** (Revelation 11:18)

Chapter 12

CURSED

Then shall he say also unto them on the **left hand**, Depart from me, ye **CURSED**, **into everlasting fire**, prepared for the devil and his angels: For I was an <u>hungred</u>, and ye gave me no meat: I was <u>thirsty</u>, and ye gave me no drink: I was a <u>stranger</u>, and ye took me not in: <u>naked</u>, and ye clothed me not: <u>sick</u>, and <u>in prison</u>, and ye visited me not. Then shall they also answer him, saying, Lord, when saw we thee an hungred, or athirst, or a stranger, or naked, or sick, or in prison, and did not minister unto thee? Then shall he answer them, saying, Verily I say unto you, <u>Inasmuch as ye did it *not* to one of the least of these, ye did it *not* to me</u>. And these shall go away into **everlasting punishment**: *but the righteous into life eternal.* (Matthew 25:41-46)

But these, as natural <u>brute beasts</u>, made to be taken and destroyed, <u>speak evil of the things that they understand not</u>; and **shall utterly perish in their own corruption; And shall receive the reward of unrighteousness,** as they that <u>count it pleasure to riot in the day time</u>. Spots they are and blemishes, sporting themselves with their <u>own deceivings</u> while they feast with you; Having eyes full of <u>adultery</u>, and **that cannot cease from sin;** <u>beguiling unstable souls</u>: an heart they have exercised with <u>covetous practices</u>; **CURSED** children: Which <u>have forsaken the right way</u>, and are <u>gone astray</u>, following the way of Balaam the son of Bosor, who

***loved* the wages of unrighteousness;** (2 Peter 2:12-15)

Chapter 13

UNQUENCHABLE FIRE

And now also the axe is laid unto the root of the trees: **therefore every tree which bringeth not forth good fruit is hewn down, and cast into the fire.** I indeed baptize you with water unto repentance. but he that cometh after me is mightier than I, whose shoes I am not worthy to bear: *he shall baptize you with the Holy Ghost, and with fire:* Whose fan is in his hand, and *he will throughly purge his floor,* and gather his wheat into the garner; but **he will burn up the chaff with UNQUENCHABLE FIRE.** (Matthew 3:10-12)

John answered, saying unto them all, I indeed baptize you with water; but one mightier than I cometh, the latchet of whose shoes I am not worthy to unloose: *he shall baptize you with the Holy Ghost and with fire:* Whose fan is in his hand, and *he will throughly purge his floor,* and will gather the wheat into his garner; but **the chaff he will burn with FIRE UNQUENCHABLE.** (Luke 3:16-17)

Chapter 14

DAMNATION

*But he that is **greatest** among you shall be your servant.* And **whosoever shall exalt himself shall be abased**; and *he that shall **humble** himself shall be **exalted**.* But *woe* unto you, scribes and Pharisees, hypocrites! for ye shut up the kingdom of heaven against men: for ye neither go in yourselves, neither suffer ye them that are entering to go in. *Woe* unto you, scribes and Pharisees, hypocrites! for ye devour widows' houses, and for a pretence make long prayer: therefore ye shall receive the **greater DAMNATION**. (Matthew 23:11-14)

Woe unto you, scribes and Pharisees, hypocrites! for ye are like unto whited sepulchres, which indeed **appear beautiful outward,** *but* **are within full of dead men's bones, and of all uncleanness.** Even so **ye also outwardly appear righteous unto men, but within ye are full of hypocrisy and iniquity.** *Woe* unto you, scribes and Pharisees, hypocrites! because ye build the tombs of the prophets, and garnish the sepulchres of the righteous, And say, If we had been in the days of our fathers, we would not have been partakers with them in the blood of the prophets. Wherefore ye be witnesses unto yourselves, that ye are the children of them which killed the prophets. Fill ye up then the measure of your fathers. Ye **serpents**, ye generation of **vipers**, how can ye escape the **DAMNATION** of hell? (Matthew 23:27-33)

But he that shall **blaspheme against the Holy Ghost hath *never* forgiveness**, but is in danger of eternal **DAMNATION**. (Mark 3:29)

And he said unto them in his doctrine, **Beware of the scribes,** which love to go in long clothing, and love salutations in the marketplaces, And the chief seats in the synagogues, and the uppermost rooms at feasts: Which devour widows' houses, and for a pretence make long prayers: these shall receive **greater DAMNATION.** (Mark 12:38-40)

He that believeth and is baptized shall be saved; but **he that believeth *not* shall be DAMNED.** (Mark 16:16)

Then in the audience of all the people he said unto his disciples, **Beware of the scribes,** which desire to walk in long robes, and love greetings in the markets, and the highest seats in the synagogues, and the chief rooms at feasts; Which devour widows' houses, and for a shew make long prayers: the same shall receive **greater DAMNATION.** (Luke 20:45-47)

Verily, verily, I say unto you, *He that heareth my*

DAMNATION / 65

word, and believeth on him that sent me, hath ***everlasting life****,* and shall not come into condemnation; but is passed from death unto life. Verily, verily, I say unto you, The hour is coming, and now is, when the dead shall hear the voice of the Son of God: and ***they that <u>hear</u> shall live.*** For as *the Father hath life in himself; so hath he given to the Son to have life in himself;* And <u>*hath given him authority to execute judgment*</u> also, because he is the Son of man. Marvel not at this: for the hour is coming, in the which all that are in the graves shall hear his voice, And shall come forth; they that have ***<u>done good</u>****,* ***unto the resurrection of life;*** and they that have ***done evil****,* **unto the resurrection of DAMNATION**. (John 5:24-29)

For if the truth of God hath more abounded through my lie unto his glory; why yet am I also judged as a sinner? And not rather, (as we be slanderously reported, and as some affirm that we say,) <u>Let us do evil, that good may come</u>? **whose DAMNATION is just.** (Romans 3:7-8)

For I have received of the Lord that which also I delivered unto you, that the Lord Jesus the same night in which he was betrayed took bread: And when he had given thanks, he brake it, and said, Take, eat: this is my body, which is broken for you: this do in remembrance of me. After the same manner also he took the cup, when he had supped, saying, this cup is the new testament in my blood: this do ye, as oft as ye drink it, in remembrance of me. For as often as ye eat this bread, and drink this cup, ye do shew the Lord's death till he come.

DAMNATION / 66

Wherefore whosoever shall eat this bread, and drink this cup of the Lord, *__unworthily,__* **shall be guilty of the body and blood of the Lord.** But let a man *examine himself,* and so let him eat of that bread, and drink of that cup. **For he that eateth and drinketh** *__unworthily__***,** eateth and drinketh **DAMNATION to himself, not discerning the Lord's body.** For this cause many are weak and sickly among you, and many sleep. (1 Corinthians 11:23-30)

For the mystery of iniquity doth already work: only he who now letteth will let, until he be taken out of the way. And then shall that Wicked be revealed, whom the Lord shall consume with the spirit of his mouth, and shall destroy with the brightness of his coming: Even him, whose coming is after the **working of Satan** with all power and signs and *lying* wonders. And with *all deceivableness* of unrighteousness in them that perish; **because they received *not* the love of the truth,** that they might be saved. And for this cause God shall send them strong delusion, that they should believe a lie: That they all might be **DAMNED** who believed *not* the truth, but **had pleasure in unrighteousness**. (2 Thessalonians 2:7-12)

Having **DAMNATION**, because they have **cast off their first faith.** (1 Timothy 5:12)

But there were **false prophets** also among the people, even as there shall be **false teachers** among you, who privily **shall bring in DAMNABLE heresies**, even denying the Lord that bought them, and bring upon themselves swift destruction. And ***many* shall follow their pernicious ways**; by reason of whom the way of truth shall be evil spoken of. And through covetousness shall they with feigned words make merchandise of you: whose judgment now of a long time lingereth not, and their **DAMNATION** slumbereth not. (2 Peter 2:1-3)

Chapter 15

DEATH

And the brother shall deliver up the brother to **DEATH**, and the father the child: and the children shall rise up against their parents, and cause them to be put to **DEATH**. And *ye shall be hated of all men for my name's sake: **but he that endureth to the end shall be saved.*** But when they persecute you in this city, flee ye into another: for verily I say unto you, Ye shall not have gone over the cities of Israel, till the Son of man be come. The disciple is not above his master, nor the servant above his lord. It is enough for the disciple that he be as his master, and the servant as his lord. If they have called the master of the house Beelzebub, how much more shall they call them of his household? *Fear them not* therefore: for there is nothing covered, that shall not be revealed; and hid, that shall not be known. What I tell you in darkness, that speak ye in light: and what ye hear in the ear, that preach ye upon the housetops. And fear not them which kill the body, but are not able to kill the soul: but rather *fear him which is able to destroy both soul and body in hell.* (Matthew 10:21-28)

For God commanded, saying, *Honour thy father and mother:* and, **He that curseth father or mother, let him die the DEATH**. (Matthew 15:4)

For Moses said, *Honour thy father and thy mother;* and, **Whoso curseth father or mother**, let him die the **DEATH**: (Mark 7:10)

And the gospel must first be published among *all* nations. But when they shall lead you, and deliver you up, take no thought beforehand what ye shall speak, neither do ye premeditate: but whatsoever shall be given you in that hour, that speak ye: for it is not ye that speak, but the Holy Ghost. Now the brother shall betray the brother to **DEATH**, and the father the son; and children shall rise up against their parents, and shall cause them to be put to **DEATH**. And *ye shall be hated of all men for my name's sake:* **but he that shall endure unto the end, the same shall be saved.** (Mark 13:10-13)

To give *light* to them that **sit in darkness** and in the **shadow of DEATH**, to *guide our feet* into the way of peace. (Luke 1:79)

And he said, *Take heed that ye **be not deceived**:* for many shall come in my name, saying, I am Christ; and the time draweth near: go ye not therefore after them. But when ye shall hear of wars and commotions, be not terrified: for these things must first come to pass; but the end is not by and by. Then said he unto them, Nation shall rise against nation, and kingdom against kingdom: And great earthquakes shall be in divers places, and famines, and pestilences; and fearful sights and great signs shall there be from heaven. But before all these, they shall lay their hands on you, and persecute you, delivering you up to the synagogues, and into prisons, being brought before kings and rulers for my name's sake. And it shall turn to you for a testimony. Settle it therefore in your hearts, not to meditate before what ye shall answer: *For I will give you a mouth and wisdom,* which all your adversaries shall not be able to gainsay nor resist. And ye shall be betrayed both by parents, and brethren, and kinsfolks, and friends; and some of you shall they cause to be put to **DEATH**. And ye shall be hated of all men for my name's sake. But there shall not an hair of your head perish. In your patience *possess ye your souls.* (Luke 21:8-19)

For this cause **God gave them up** unto vile affections: for even their women did change the natural use into that which is against nature: And likewise also the men, leaving the natural use of the woman, burned in their lust one toward another; men with men working that which is unseemly, and receiving in themselves that recompence of their error which was meet. And even as they did not like to retain God in their knowledge, **God gave them over to a reprobate mind,** to do those things which are not convenient; Being filled with all unrighteousness, fornication, wickedness, covetousness, maliciousness; full of envy, murder, debate, deceit, malignity; whisperers, Backbiters, haters of God, despiteful, proud, boasters, inventors of evil things, disobedient to parents, Without understanding, covenantbreakers, without natural affection, implacable, unmerciful: Who knowing ***the judgment of God,*** that they which commit such things are **worthy of DEATH**, not only do the same, but have pleasure in them that do them. (Romans 1:26-32)

Wherefore, as by one man sin entered into the world, and **DEATH** by sin; and so **DEATH** passed upon all men, for that **all have sinned:** (Romans 5:12)

That as **sin hath reigned unto DEATH**, even so might *grace reign through righteousness* unto eternal life by Jesus Christ our Lord. (Romans 5:21)

Likewise reckon ye also yourselves to be **DEAD indeed unto sin**, *but alive unto God* through Jesus Christ our Lord. **Let *not* sin therefore reign in your mortal body, that ye should obey it in the lusts thereof.** *Neither* yield ye your members as instruments of unrighteousness unto sin: but *yield yourselves unto God,* as those that are alive from the dead, and your members as instruments of righteousness unto God. *For sin shall* ***not*** *have dominion over you*: for ye are not under the law, but under grace. What then? shall we sin, because we are not under the law, but under grace? *God forbid.* Know ye not, that to whom ye yield yourselves servants to obey, his servants ye are to whom ye obey; whether of **sin unto DEATH**, or of *obedience unto righteousness?* (Romans 6:11-16)

What fruit had ye then in those things whereof ye are now ashamed? for the end of those things is **DEATH**. But now being made *free from sin,* and become *servants to God,* ye have your fruit unto holiness, and the end everlasting life. **For the wages of sin is DEATH**; but the gift of God is eternal life through Jesus Christ our Lord. (Romans 6:21-23)

For when we were in the flesh, the motions of sins, which were by the law, did work in our members to **bring forth fruit unto DEATH.** (Romans 7:5)

For I was alive without the law once: but when the commandment came, sin revived, and I died. And the commandment, which was ordained to life, I found to be unto **DEATH.** For <u>sin</u>, taking occasion by the commandment, **deceived me, and by it slew me.** Wherefore *the law is holy, and the commandment holy, and just, and good.* Was then that which is good made death unto me? *God forbid.* But <u>sin</u>, that it might appear sin, working **DEATH** in me by that which is good; that sin by the commandment might become exceeding sinful. For we know that *the law is spiritual:* but I am carnal, sold under sin. For that which I do I allow not: for what I would, that do I not; but what I hate, that do I. If then I do that which I would not, I consent unto the law that it is good. Now then it is no more I that do it, but sin that dwelleth in me. <u>For I know that in me (that is, in my flesh,) dwelleth no good thing</u>: for to will is present with me; but how to perform that which is good I find not. For the good that I would I do not: but the evil which I would not, that I do. Now if I do that I would not, it is no more I that do it, but sin that dwelleth in me. I find then a law, that, when I would do good, evil is present with me. (Romans 7:9-21)

O wretched man that I am! who shall deliver me from the body of this **DEATH**? (Romans 7:24)

For **to be <u>carnally minded</u> is DEATH**; but to be *spiritually minded is life and peace.* (Romans 8:6)

The **last enemy** that shall be destroyed is **DEATH**. (1 Corinthians 15:26)

The sting of DEATH is sin; and the strength of sin is the law. (1 Corinthians 15:56)

To the one we are the **savour of DEATH unto DEATH**; and to the other the *savour of life unto life.* And who is sufficient for these things? (2 Corinthians 2:16)

For though I made you sorry with a letter, I do not repent, though I did repent: for I perceive that the same epistle hath made you sorry, though it were but for a season. Now I rejoice, not that ye were made sorry, but that *ye sorrowed to repentance*: for ye were made sorry after a godly manner, that ye might receive damage by us in nothing. For *godly sorrow worketh repentance to salvation* not to be repented of: but **the sorrow of the world worketh DEATH**. (2 Corinthians 7:8-10)

Blessed is the man that endureth temptation: for when he is tried, he shall receive the *crown of life*, which the Lord hath promised to them that *love him*. Let no man say when he is tempted, I am tempted of God: for God cannot be tempted with evil, neither tempteth he any man: But every man is tempted, when he is drawn away of his own lust, and enticed. Then when lust hath conceived, it bringeth forth sin: and **sin, when it is finished, bringeth forth DEATH**. (James 1:12-15)

We know that we have passed from **DEATH** unto life, *because we love the brethren*. **He that loveth *not* his brother** abideth in DEATH. (1 John 3:14)

If any man see his brother sin a sin which is not unto **DEATH**, he shall ask, and he shall give him life for them that sin not unto **DEATH**. There is a sin unto **DEATH**: I do not say that he shall pray for it. **All unrighteousness is sin:** and there is a sin not unto **DEATH**. We know that *whosoever is born of God sinneth **not***; but he that is begotten of God *keepeth himself*, and that wicked one toucheth him not. (1 John 5:16-18)

I am he that liveth, and was dead; and, behold, I am alive for evermore, Amen; and have the **keys of hell and of DEATH**. (Revelation 1:18)

Fear none of those things which thou shalt suffer: behold, <u>the devil</u> shall cast some of you into prison, that ye may be tried; and ye shall have tribulation ten days: *be thou faithful unto* **DEATH**, *and I will give thee a crown of life.* He that hath an ear, let him hear what the Spirit saith unto the churches; ***He that*** <u>***overcometh***</u> ***shall not be hurt of the second*** **DEATH.** (Revelation 2:10-11)

And unto the angel of the <u>church in Thyatira</u> write; These things saith the Son of God, who hath his eyes like unto a flame of fire, and his feet are like fine brass; I know thy works, and charity, and service, and faith, and thy patience, and thy works; and the last to be more than the first. *Notwithstanding* I have a few things against thee, because **thou sufferest that woman Jezebel, which** *calleth* **herself a prophetess, to teach and to** <u>**seduce my servants to commit fornication**</u>**, and to eat things sacrificed unto idols.** And I gave her space to repent of her <u>fornication</u>; and <u>she repented not</u>. Behold, I will cast her into a bed, and them that commit adultery with her into great tribulation, *except they repent of their deeds.* And I will kill her children with **DEATH**; and all the churches shall know that *I am he which searcheth the reins and hearts: and I will give unto every one of you according to your works.* (Revelation 2:18-23)

And when he had opened the <u>fourth seal</u>, I heard the voice of the <u>fourth beast</u> say, Come and see. And I looked, and behold **a pale horse**: and his name that sat on him was **DEATH**, and Hell followed with him. And power was given unto them over the fourth part of the earth, **to kill with sword, and with hunger, and with DEATH, and with the beasts of the earth.** (Revelation 6:7-8)

And the fifth angel sounded, and I saw *a star fall* from heaven unto the earth: and to him was given the key of the bottomless pit. And he opened the bottomless pit; and there arose a smoke out of the pit, as the smoke of a great furnace; and the sun and the air were darkened by reason of the smoke of the pit. And there came out of the smoke **locusts** upon the earth: and unto them was given power, as the scorpions of the earth have power. And it was commanded them that they should not hurt the grass of the earth, neither any green thing, neither any tree; but only those men which have *not* the seal of God in their foreheads. And to them it was given that they should not kill them, but that they should be **tormented five months:** and their torment was as the torment of a scorpion, when he striketh a man. And in those days **shall men seek DEATH, and shall not find it**; and shall desire to die, and **DEATH** shall flee from them. (Revelation 9:1-6)

And after these things I saw another angel come down from heaven, having great power; and the earth was lightened with his glory. And he cried mightily with a strong voice, saying, **Babylon** the great is fallen, is fallen, and is become the habitation of devils, and the hold of every foul spirit, and a cage of every unclean and hateful bird. For all nations have drunk of the wine of the wrath of **her fornication**, and the **kings** of the earth have committed fornication with her, and the **merchants** of the earth are waxed rich through the abundance of her delicacies. And I heard another voice from heaven, saying, **Come out of her, my people, that ye be not partakers of her sins, and that ye receive not of her plagues.** For her sins have reached unto heaven, and God hath remembered her iniquities. Reward her even as she rewarded you, and double unto her double according to her works: in the cup which she hath filled fill to her double. How much she hath glorified herself, and lived deliciously, so much torment and sorrow give her: for she saith in her heart, **I sit a queen**, and am no widow, and shall see no sorrow. Therefore shall her plagues come in one day, DEATH, and mourning, and famine; and she shall be utterly burned with fire: for strong is the Lord God who judgeth her. And the **kings** of the earth, who have committed fornication *and* lived deliciously with her, shall bewail her, and lament for her, when they shall see the smoke of her burning, Standing afar off for the fear of her torment, saying, **Alas, alas that great city Babylon, that mighty city! for in one hour is thy judgment come.** And **the merchants** of the earth shall weep and mourn over her; for no man buyeth their merchandise any more: (Revelation 18:1-11)

And I saw a *great white throne*, and him that sat on it, from whose face the earth and the heaven fled away; and there was found **no place for them**. And I saw the dead, small and great, stand before God; and the books were opened: and another book was opened, which is the book of life: and the dead were judged out of those things which were written in the books, *according to their works.* And the sea gave up the dead which were in it; and **DEATH** and hell delivered up the dead which were in them: and they were *judged every man according to their works.* And **DEATH** and hell were cast into the lake of fire. This is the second **DEATH**. **And whosoever was *not* found written in the <u>book of life</u> was cast into the lake of fire.** (Revelation 20:11-15)

But the <u>fearful</u>, and <u>unbelieving</u>, and the <u>abominable</u>, and <u>murderers</u>, and <u>whoremongers</u>, and <u>sorcerers</u>, and <u>idolaters</u>, and *<u>all liars</u>,* shall have their part in the lake which burneth with fire and brimstone: which is **the second DEATH**. (Revelation 21:8)

Chapter 16

FEAR

And the brother shall deliver up the brother to death, and the father the child: and the children shall rise up against their parents, and cause them to be put to death. And ye shall be *hated* of all men for my name's sake: but *he that endureth to the end* shall be saved. But when they persecute you in this city, flee ye into another: for verily I say unto you, Ye shall not have gone over the cities of Israel, till the Son of man be come. The disciple is not above his master, nor the servant above his lord. It is enough for the disciple that he be as his master, and the servant as his lord. If they have called the master of the house Beelzebub, how much more shall they call them of his household? **FEAR** them *not* therefore: for there is nothing covered, that shall not be revealed; and hid, that shall not be known. What I tell you in darkness, that speak ye in light: and what ye hear in the ear, that preach ye upon the housetops. And **FEAR** *not* them which kill the body, but are not able to kill the soul: but rather **FEAR** *him which is able to destroy both soul and body in hell.* (Matthew 10:21-28)

And he said unto them, **Why are ye so FEARFUL?** how is it that ye have *no faith*? (Mark 4:40)

And *his mercy is on them that* **FEAR** *him* from generation to generation. (Luke 1:50)

And I say unto you my friends, Be not afraid of them that kill the body, and after that have no more that they can do. But I will forewarn you whom ye shall fear: **FEAR** *him, which after he hath killed hath power to cast into hell;* yea, I say unto you, **FEAR** *him.* (Luke 12:4-5)

And as they heard these things, he added and spake a parable, because he was nigh to Jerusalem, and because they thought that the kingdom of God should immediately appear. He said therefore, A certain nobleman went into a far country to receive for himself a kingdom, and to return. And he called his **ten servants**, and delivered them **ten pounds**, and said unto them, *Occupy till I come.* But his citizens hated him, and sent a message after him, saying, We will not have this man to reign over us. And it came to pass, that when he was returned, having received the kingdom, then *he commanded these servants to be called unto him, to whom he had given the money, that he might know how much every man had gained by trading.* Then came the *first*, saying, Lord, *thy pound hath gained ten pounds.* And he said unto him, *Well, thou good servant:* because thou hast been faithful in a very little, have thou authority over ten cities. And the *second* came, saying, Lord, thy pound hath gained *five pounds.* And he said likewise to him, Be thou also over five cities. And *another* came, saying, Lord, behold, here is thy pound, which I have kept laid up in a napkin: **For I FEARED thee,** *because thou art an austere man:* thou takest up that thou layedst not down, and reapest that thou didst not sow. And he saith unto him, **Out of thine own mouth will I judge thee, thou wicked servant.** *Thou knewest that I was an austere man,* taking up that I laid not down, and reaping that I did not sow: Wherefore then gavest not thou my money into the bank, that at my coming I might have required mine own with usury? And he said unto them that stood by, Take from him the pound, and give it to him that hath ten pounds. (And they said unto him, Lord, he hath ten pounds.) For I say unto you, That unto every one which hath shall be given; and from him that hath not, even that he hath shall be taken away from him. But *those mine enemies, which would not that I should reign over them, bring hither, and slay them before me.* (Luke 19:11-27)

And they asked him, saying, Master, but when shall these things be? and what sign will there be when these things shall come to pass? And he said, *Take heed that ye be not deceived:* **for many shall come in my name, saying, I am Christ;** and the time draweth near: go ye not therefore after them. But when ye shall hear of wars and commotions, be not terrified: for these things must first come to pass; but the end is not by and by. Then said he unto them, Nation shall rise against nation, and kingdom against kingdom: And great earthquakes shall be in divers places, and famines, and pestilences; and **FEARFUL** sights and great signs shall there be from heaven. But before all these, they shall lay their hands on you, and persecute you, delivering you up to the synagogues, and into prisons, being brought before kings and rulers for my name's sake. (Luke 21:7-12)

And one of the malefactors which were hanged railed on him, saying, If thou be Christ, save thyself and us. But the other answering rebuked him, saying, ***Dost not thou* FEAR *God,*** seeing thou art in the same condemnation? And we indeed justly; for we receive the due reward of our deeds: but this man hath done nothing amiss. (Luke 23:39-41)

Then Peter said unto them, **Repent, and be baptized every one of you in the name of Jesus Christ** for the remission of sins, *and* ye shall receive the gift of the Holy Ghost. For the promise is unto you, and to your children, and to all that are afar off, even as many as the LORD our God shall call. And with many other words did he testify and exhort, saying, ***Save yourselves*** from this untoward generation. Then they that gladly received his word were baptized: and the same day there were added unto them about three thousand souls. And they continued stedfastly in the apostles' doctrine and fellowship, and in breaking of bread, and in prayers. And **FEAR** came upon every soul: and many wonders and signs were done by the apostles. (Acts 2:38-43)

But a certain man named Ananias, with Sapphira his wife, sold a possession, And kept back part of the price, his wife also being privy to it, and brought a certain part, and laid it at the apostles' feet. But Peter said, Ananias, <u>why hath Satan filled thine heart to *lie* to the Holy Ghost</u>, and to keep back part of the price of the land? Whiles it remained, was it not thine own? and after it was sold, was it not in thine own power? why hast thou conceived this thing in thine heart? **thou hast not lied unto men, but unto God.** And Ananias hearing these words fell down, and gave up the ghost: and great **FEAR** came on all them that heard these things. And the young men arose, wound him up, and carried him out, and buried him. And it was about the space of three hours after, when his wife, not knowing what was done, came in. And Peter answered unto her, Tell me whether ye sold the land for so much? And she said, Yea, for so much. Then Peter said unto her, <u>How is it that ye have agreed together to **tempt** the Spirit of the Lord</u>? behold, the feet of them which have buried thy husband are at the door, and shall carry thee out. Then fell she down straightway at his feet, and yielded up the ghost: and the young men came in, and found her dead, and, carrying her forth, buried her by her husband. And great **FEAR** came upon all the church, and upon as many as heard these things. (Acts 5:1-11)

There was a certain man in Caesarea called Cornelius, a centurion of the band called the Italian band, A devout man, and **one that FEARED God with all his house,** which gave *much alms* to the people, and *prayed to God alway*. (Acts 10:1-2)

And they said, Cornelius the centurion, *a just man,* and **one that FEARETH God,** and of *good report* among all the nation of the Jews, was warned from God by an holy angel to send for thee into his house, and to hear words of thee. (Acts 10:22)

Then Peter opened his mouth, and said, Of a truth I perceive that God is no respecter of persons: But in every nation **he that FEARETH him,** *and **worketh righteousness,*** is accepted with him. (Acts 10:34-45)

Men and brethren, children of the stock of Abraham, and whosoever among you **FEARETH God***,* to you is the word of this salvation sent. (Acts 13:26)

Then certain of the vagabond Jews, exorcists, took upon them to call over them which had evil spirits the name of the LORD Jesus, saying, We adjure you by Jesus whom Paul preacheth. And there were seven sons of one Sceva, a Jew, and chief of the priests, which did so. And the evil spirit answered and said, Jesus I know, and Paul I know; but who are ye? And the man in whom the evil spirit was leaped on them, and overcame them, and prevailed against them, so that they fled out of that house naked and wounded. And this was known to all the Jews and Greeks also dwelling at Ephesus; and **FEAR** fell on them all, and ***the name of the Lord Jesus was magnified.*** And many that believed came, and confessed, and shewed their deeds. *Many of them also which used curious arts brought their books together, and burned them* before all men: and they counted the price of them, and found it fifty thousand pieces of silver. (Acts 19:13-19)

As it is written, There is none righteous, no, not one: <u>There is none that understandeth</u>, <u>there is none that seeketh after God</u>. They are all <u>gone out of the way</u>, they are together <u>become unprofitable</u>; there is <u>none that doeth good</u>, no, not one. Their throat is an open sepulchre; with their <u>tongues they have used deceit</u>; the poison of asps is under their lips: Whose <u>mouth is full of cursing and bitterness</u>: Their <u>feet are swift to shed blood</u>: <u>Destruction and misery are in their ways</u>: And the way of peace have they not known: ***There is* FEAR *of God before their eyes.*** (Romans 3:10-18)

And if some of the branches be broken off, and thou, being a wild olive tree, wert grafted in among them, and with them partakest of the root and fatness of the olive tree; Boast not against the branches. But if thou boast, thou bearest not the root, but the root thee. Thou wilt say then, The branches were broken off, that I might be grafted in. Well; because of unbelief they were broken off, and thou standest by faith. Be not highminded, but **FEAR**: For if God spared not the natural branches, take heed lest he also spare not thee. ***Behold therefore the goodness and severity of God:* <u>on them which fell</u>, severity;** *<u>but toward thee, goodness</u>, <u>if</u> thou continue in his goodness:* **otherwise thou also shalt be cut off.** (Romans 11:17-22)

Having therefore these promises, dearly beloved, *let us cleanse ourselves* from all filthiness of the flesh and spirit, *perfecting holiness* in the **FEAR** of God. (2 Corinthians 7:1)

For I am jealous over you with godly jealousy: for I have espoused you to one husband, *that I may present you as a chaste virgin to Christ.* But I **FEAR**, lest by any means, as the serpent beguiled Eve through his subtilty, so your minds should be corrupted from the simplicity that is in Christ. For if he that cometh preacheth *another* Jesus, whom we have not preached, or if ye receive another spirit, which ye have not received, or another gospel, which ye have not accepted, ye might well bear with him. (2 Corinthians 11:2-4)

For I **FEAR**, lest, when I come, I shall not find you such as I would, and that I shall be found unto you such as ye would not: lest there be debates, envyings, wraths, strifes, backbitings, whisperings, swellings, tumults: And lest, when I come again, my God will humble me among you, and that I shall bewail many which have sinned already, and **have not repented of the** uncleanness and fornication and lasciviousness **which they have committed.** (2 Corinthians 12:20)

Submitting yourselves *one to another* in the **FEAR** of God. Wives, submit yourselves unto your own husbands, as unto the Lord. For the husband is the head of the wife, even as Christ is the head of the church: and he is the saviour of the body. Therefore as the church is subject unto Christ, so let the wives be to their own husbands in every thing. Husbands, love your wives, even as Christ also loved the church, and gave himself for it; *That he might sanctify and cleanse it* with the washing of water by the word, **That he might present it to himself a glorious church, not having spot, or wrinkle, or any such thing; but that it should be holy and without blemish.** So ought men to love their wives as their own bodies. He that loveth his wife loveth himself. (Ephesians 5:21-28)

Wherefore God also hath highly exalted him, and given him a name which is above every name: That at the name of Jesus every knee should bow, of things in heaven, and things in earth, and things under the earth; And that every tongue should confess that <u>***Jesus Christ***</u> is Lord, to the glory of God the Father. Wherefore, my beloved, as ye have always obeyed, not as in my presence only, but now much more in my absence, *work out your own salvation with* **FEAR** *and trembling*. (Phillipians 2:9-12)

Against *an elder* receive not an accusation, but before two or three witnesses. <u>**Them that sin rebuke before all**</u>**,** that others also may **FEAR.** (1 Timothy 5:19-20)

Let us therefore FEAR, lest, a promise being left us of entering into his rest, <u>any of you should seem to *come short* of it</u>. (Hebrews 4:1)

For if we sin *wilfully* after that we have received the knowledge of the truth, **there remaineth no more sacrifice for sins,** But a certain **FEARFUL** looking for of **judgment and fiery indignation**, which shall devour the adversaries. He that despised Moses' law died without mercy under two or three witnesses: **Of how much sorer punishment**, suppose ye, shall he be thought worthy, who hath trodden under foot the Son of God, and hath counted the blood of the covenant, wherewith he was sanctified, an unholy thing, and hath done despite unto the Spirit of grace? For we know him that hath said, **Vengeance belongeth unto me, I will recompense,** saith the Lord. And again, The Lord shall judge his people. *It is a* **FEARFUL** *thing to fall into the hands of the living God.* (Hebrews 10:26-31)

By faith *Noah,* being warned of God of things not seen as yet, moved with **FEAR**, prepared an ark to the saving of his house; *by the which he condemned the world,* and became heir of the righteousness which is by faith. (Hebrews 11:7)

Looking diligently lest any man fail of the grace of God; lest any root of bitterness springing up trouble you, and thereby many be defiled; Lest there be any fornicator, or profane person, as **Esau**, who for one morsel of meat sold his birthright. For ye know how that afterward, when he would have inherited the blessing, **he was rejected: for he found *no* place of repentance, though he sought it carefully with tears.** For ye are not come unto the mount that might be touched, and that burned with fire, nor unto blackness, and darkness, and tempest, And the sound of a trumpet, and the voice of words; which voice they that heard intreated that the word should not be spoken to them any more: (For they could not endure that which was commanded, And if so much as a beast touch the mountain, it shall be stoned, or thrust through with a dart: And so terrible was the sight, that Moses said, I exceedingly **FEAR** and quake:) (Hebrews 12:15-21)

To the general assembly and church of the firstborn, which are written in heaven, and to God the Judge of all, and to the spirits of just men made perfect, And to Jesus the mediator of the new covenant, and to the blood of sprinkling, that speaketh better things than that of Abel. <u>See that ye *refuse not* him that speaketh</u>. **For if <u>they</u> escaped *not* who refused him that spake on earth, much more shall *not* <u>we</u> escape, if we turn away from him that speaketh from heaven:** Whose voice then shook the earth: but now he hath promised, saying, Yet once more I shake not the earth only, but also heaven. And this word, Yet once more, signifieth the removing of those things that are shaken, as of things that are made, that those things which cannot be shaken may remain. *Wherefore we receiving a kingdom which cannot be moved,* let us have grace, whereby *we may serve God acceptably with reverence and godly* **FEAR**: ***For our God is a consuming fire.*** (Hebrews 12:23-29)

As *obedient children*, ***not*** fashioning yourselves according to the <u>former lusts</u> in your ignorance: But as he which hath called you is holy, so be ye holy in all manner of conversation; Because it is written, **Be ye holy; for I am holy.** And if ye call on the Father, who without respect of persons *judgeth according to every man's work,* **pass the time of your sojourning here in FEAR**: (1 Peter 1:14-17)

Honour all men. Love the brotherhood. **FEAR God.** Honour the king. (1 Peter 2:17)

Likewise, ye wives, be in subjection to your own husbands; that, if any obey not the word, they also may without the word be *won by the conversation of the wives;* While they behold your **chaste conversation** <u>**coupled**</u> **with FEAR.** (1 Peter 3:1-2)

But sanctify the Lord God in your hearts: and *be ready always to give an answer* to every man that asketh you a reason of the hope that is in you with meekness and **FEAR:** Having a good conscience; that, whereas they speak evil of you, as of evildoers, they may be ashamed that falsely accuse your good conversation in Christ. *For it is better, if the will of God be so, that ye suffer for well doing, than for evil doing.* (1 Peter 3:15-17)

But these <u>speak evil of those things which they know not</u>: but what they know naturally, as brute beasts, in those things **they corrupt themselves**. *Woe* unto them! for they have gone in the way of Cain, and ran greedily after the error of Balaam for reward, and perished in the gainsaying of Core. These are spots in your feasts of charity, when they feast with you, feeding themselves <u>without</u> **FEAR:**

clouds they are without water, carried about of winds; trees whose fruit withereth, without fruit, twice dead, plucked up by the roots; Raging waves of the sea, foaming out their own shame; wandering stars, **to whom is reserved the blackness of darkness for ever.** (Jude 1:10-13)

But, beloved, remember ye the words which were spoken before of the apostles of our Lord Jesus Christ; How that they told you there should be mockers in the last time, who should walk after their own ungodly lusts. These be they who separate themselves, sensual, having not the Spirit. But ye, beloved, building up yourselves on your most holy faith, praying in the Holy Ghost, Keep yourselves in the love of God, looking for the mercy of our Lord Jesus Christ unto eternal life. And of some have compassion, making a difference: And **others save with FEAR, pulling them out of the fire;** hating even the garment spotted by the flesh. (Jude 1:17-23)

Unto the angel of the *church of Ephesus* write; These things saith he that holdeth the seven stars in his right hand, who walketh in the midst of the seven golden candlesticks; I know thy works, and thy labour, and thy patience, and *how thou canst not bear them which are evil:* and thou hast tried them which say they are apostles, and are not, and hast **found them liars:** And hast borne, and hast patience, and *for my name's sake hast laboured, and hast not fainted.* **Nevertheless** I have somewhat against thee, because **thou hast left thy first love.** Remember therefore from whence thou art fallen, and *repent, and do the first works;* ***or else*** I will come unto thee quickly, and will remove thy candlestick out of his place, **except thou repent. But this thou hast, that thou hatest the deeds of the Nicolaitanes, which I also hate.** He that hath an ear, let him hear what the Spirit saith unto the churches; To him that ***overcometh*** will I give to eat of the tree of life, which is in the midst of the paradise of God. And unto the angel of the <u>church in Smyrna</u> write; These things saith the first and the last, which was dead, and is alive; *I know thy works, and tribulation, and poverty,* (but thou art rich) and <u>I know the blasphemy of them which say they are Jews, and are not, but are the synagogue of Satan</u>. **FEAR** *none of those things which thou shalt suffer:* behold, the devil shall cast some of you into prison, that ye may be tried; and ye shall have tribulation ten days: ***be thou faithful unto death****, and I will give thee a crown of life.* He that hath an ear, let him hear what the Spirit saith unto the churches; He that ***overcometh*** shall not be hurt of the second death. (Revelation 2:1-11)

And I will give power unto ***my two witnesses***, and they shall prophesy a thousand two hundred and threescore days, clothed in sackcloth. These are the ***two olive trees****,* and the ***two candlesticks*** <u>**standing before the God of the earth.**</u> And if any man will hurt them, *fire proceedeth out of their mouth*, and devoureth their enemies: and if any man will hurt them, he must in this manner be killed. These have <u>power to shut heaven</u>, that it rain not in the days of their prophecy: and have <u>power over waters to turn them to blood</u>, and <u>to smite the earth with all</u>

plagues, as often as they will. And when they shall have finished their testimony, **the beast** that ascendeth out of the bottomless pit shall make war against them, *and* shall overcome them, *and* kill them. And their dead bodies shall lie in the street of **the great city**, which ***spiritually*** is called Sodom *and* Egypt, where also our Lord was crucified. And they of the people and kindreds and tongues and nations shall see their dead bodies three days and an half, and shall not suffer their dead bodies to be put in graves. And they that dwell upon the earth shall rejoice over them, and make merry, and shall send gifts one to another; because ***these two prophets tormented them*** that dwelt on the earth. And *after three days and an half the spirit of life from God entered into them, and they stood upon their feet;* and great **FEAR** fell upon them which saw them. And they heard a great voice from heaven saying unto them, **Come up hither.** And *they ascended up to heaven in a cloud;* and their enemies beheld them. And **the same hour** was there a great earthquake, and the tenth part of the city fell, and in the earthquake were slain of men seven thousand: and *the remnant were affrighted, and gave glory to the God of heaven.* The second woe is past; and, behold, the third woe cometh quickly. And the seventh angel sounded; and there were great voices in heaven, saying, *The kingdoms of this world are become the kingdoms of our Lord, and of his Christ; and he shall reign for ever and ever.* And the four and twenty elders, which sat before God on their seats, fell upon their faces, and worshipped God, Saying, *We give thee thanks, O L*ORD *God Almighty, which art, and wast, and art to come;*

because thou hast taken to thee thy great power, and hast reigned. And the nations were angry, and **thy wrath is come**, and the time of the dead, that **they should be judged**, and that thou shouldest give <u>reward</u> unto thy <u>servants the prophets</u>, and to the <u>saints</u>, and <u>them that fear thy name</u>, small and great; and shouldest **destroy them which destroy the earth.** And the temple of God was opened in heaven, and there was seen in his temple the ark of his testament: and there were lightnings, and voices, and thunderings, and an earthquake, and great hail. (Revelation 11:3-19)

And I saw <u>another angel</u> fly in the midst of heaven, having the **everlasting gospel** to preach unto them that dwell on the earth, and to every nation, and kindred, and tongue, and people, Saying with a loud voice, **FEAR *God, and give glory to him*;** for the hour of his judgment is come: and *worship him* that made heaven, and earth, and the sea, and the fountains of waters. (Revelation 14:6-7)

And I saw another sign in heaven, great and marvellous, <u>seven angels</u> having the **<u>seven last plagues</u>;** for ***in them is filled up the wrath of God.*** And I saw as it were a sea of glass mingled with fire: and them that had gotten the ***victory over the beast,*** and <u>over his **image**,</u> and <u>over his **mark**,</u> and <u>over the number of his **name**</u>, stand on the sea of glass, having the harps of God. And they sing the <u>song of Moses</u> the servant of God, and the <u>song of the Lamb</u>, saying, *Great and marvellous are thy works, Lord God Almighty; just and true are thy ways, thou King of saints. Who shall not* **FEAR** *thee, O Lord, and glorify thy name? for thou only art holy: for all nations shall come and worship before thee; for thy judgments are made manifest.* (Revelation 15:1-4)

And after these things I saw <u>another angel</u> come down from heaven, having great power; and the earth was lightened with his glory. And he cried mightily with a strong voice, saying, **Babylon** the great is fallen, is fallen, and is become the <u>habitation of devils</u>, and the hold of <u>every foul spirit</u>, and a cage of <u>every unclean and hateful bird</u>. For ***all* nations** <u>have drunk of the wine of the wrath of her</u> **fornication,** and the **kings** of the earth have committed **fornication** with her, and the **merchants** of the earth are **waxed rich** through the abundance of her delicacies. And I heard another voice from heaven, saying, ***Come out of her, <u>my people</u>, that ye be not partakers of her sins, and that ye receive not of her plagues.*** For her sins have reached unto heaven, and God hath remembered her iniquities. Reward her even as she rewarded you, and double unto her double according to her works: in the cup which she hath filled fill to her double. How much she hath <u>glorified herself</u>, and <u>lived deliciously</u>, so much torment and sorrow give her: for she saith in her heart, **I sit a <u>queen</u>**, and am no widow, and shall see no sorrow. Therefore shall her plagues come in one day, death, and mourning, and famine; and **she shall be utterly burned with fire: for strong is the Lord God who judgeth her.** And the kings of the earth, who have committed <u>fornication</u> and <u>lived deliciously with her</u>, shall bewail her, and lament for her, when they shall see the smoke of her burning, Standing afar off for the **FEAR** of her torment, saying, Alas, alas that great city **Babylon, that mighty city!** for **in one hour is thy judgment come.** And the merchants of the earth shall weep and mourn over her; for no man buyeth their merchandise any more: The *merchandise* of gold, and silver, and precious stones, and of pearls, and fine linen, and purple, and silk, and scarlet, and all thyine wood, and all manner vessels of ivory, and all manner vessels of most precious wood, and of brass, and iron, and marble, And cinnamon, and odours, and ointments, and frankincense, and wine, and oil, and fine flour, and wheat, and beasts, and sheep, and horses, and chariots, and slaves, and souls of men. And the fruits that thy soul lusted after are departed from thee, and all things which were dainty and goodly are departed from thee, and thou shalt find them no more at all. The merchants of these things, which were made rich by her, shall stand afar off for the **FEAR** of her torment, weeping and wailing, And saying, Alas, alas **that great city,** that was clothed in fine linen, and purple, and scarlet, and decked with gold, and precious stones, and pearls! For in one hour so great riches is come to nought. And every shipmaster, and all the company in ships, and sailors, and as many as trade by sea, stood afar off, And cried when they saw the smoke of her burning, saying, What city is like unto this great city! And they cast dust on their heads, and cried, weeping and wailing, saying, **Alas, alas that great city,** wherein were made rich all that had ships in the sea by reason of her costliness! for in one hour is she made desolate. *Rejoice over her, thou heaven, and ye holy apostles and prophets;* for

God hath avenged you on her. And a mighty angel took up a stone like a great millstone, and cast it into the sea, saying, **Thus with violence shall that great city <u>Babylon</u> be thrown down, and shall be found no more at all.** (Revelation 18:1-21)

And after these things I heard a great voice of much people in heaven, saying, *Alleluia; Salvation, and glory, and honour, and power, unto the Lord our God: For true and righteous are his judgments:* for *he hath judged* **the great whore**, <u>which did corrupt the earth with her fornication,</u> *and* <u>hath avenged the blood of his servants</u> at her hand. And again they said, *Alleluia* And her smoke rose up for ever and ever. And the *<u>four and twenty elders</u>* and *<u>the four beasts</u>* fell down and worshipped God that sat on the throne, saying, *Amen; Alleluia.* And a voice came out of the throne, saying, *Praise our God, all ye his servants, and ye that* **FEAR** *him, both small and great.* (Revelation 19:1-5)

But the **<u>FEARFUL</u>**, and <u>unbelieving</u>, and the <u>abominable</u>, and <u>murderers</u>, and <u>whoremongers</u>, and <u>sorcerers</u>, and <u>idolaters</u>, and *<u>all liars</u>*, **shall have their part in the lake which burneth with fire and brimstone: which is the second death.** (Revelation 21:8)

Chapter 17

PERISH

Ye have heard that it was said by them of old time, Thou shalt not commit <u>adultery</u>: But I say unto you, That whosoever <u>looketh on a woman to lust</u> after her hath committed adultery with her already in his heart. And <u>if thy right **eye** offend thee</u>, *pluck it out,* and cast it from thee: for *it is profitable for thee* that one of thy members should **PERISH**, and **not that thy whole body should be cast into hell.** And <u>if thy right **hand** offend thee</u>, *cut it off,* and cast it from thee: for *it is profitable for thee* that one of thy members should **PERISH**, and **not that thy whole body should be cast into hell.** (Matthew 5:27-30)

There were present at that season some that told him of the Galilaeans, whose blood Pilate had mingled with their sacrifices. And Jesus answering said unto them, Suppose ye that these Galilaeans were sinners above all the Galilaeans, because they suffered such things? I tell you, Nay: but, **except ye repent, ye shall all likewise PERISH**. Or those eighteen, upon whom the tower in Siloam fell, and slew them, think ye that they were sinners above all men that dwelt in Jerusalem? I tell you, Nay: but, **except ye repent, ye shall all likewise PERISH**. (Luke 13:1-5)

Labour *not* for the meat which **PERISHETH**, but for that *meat which endureth unto everlasting life,* which the Son of man shall give unto you: for him hath God the Father sealed. (John 6:27)

And when Simon saw that through laying on of the apostles' hands the Holy Ghost was given, he offered them money, Saying, Give me also this power, that on whomsoever I lay hands, he may receive the Holy Ghost. But Peter said unto him, Thy money **PERISH** with thee, because thou hast thought that the gift of God may be purchased with money. Thou hast neither part nor lot in this matter: for **thy heart is not right in the sight of God.** Repent therefore of this thy wickedness, and pray God, if perhaps **the thought of thine heart** may be forgiven thee. For I perceive that thou art in the gall of bitterness, and in the bond of iniquity. Then answered Simon, and said, Pray ye to the LORD for me, that none of these things which ye have spoken come upon me. (Acts 8:18-24)

Be it known unto you therefore, men and brethren, that through this man is preached unto you the forgiveness of sins: And by him (Jesus) all that believe are justified from all things, from which **ye could not be justified by the law of Moses.** *Beware* therefore, lest that come upon you, which is spoken of in the prophets; Behold, ye despisers, and wonder, and **PERISH**: for I work a work in your days, a work which ye shall in no wise believe, though a man declare it unto you. (Acts 13:38-41)

Therefore thou art inexcusable, O man, whosoever thou art that judgest: for wherein thou judgest another, thou condemnest thyself; for <u>thou that judgest doest the same things</u>. But we are sure that the judgment of God is according to truth against them which commit such things. And thinkest thou this, O man, <u>that judgest them which do such things, and doest the same</u>, that thou shalt escape the judgment of God? **Or despisest thou the riches of his goodness and forbearance and longsuffering;** *not knowing that the goodness of God leadeth thee to repentance?* But after <u>thy hardness and impenitent heart</u> treasurest up unto thyself **wrath** against the **day of wrath** and revelation of the righteous judgment of God; Who will render to every man *according to his deeds*: To them who by *patient continuance in well doing* seek for glory and honour and immortality, *eternal life:* But unto them that are <u>contentious</u>, and <u>do not obey the truth</u>, but <u>obey unrighteousness</u>, **indignation** *and* **wrath**, **Tribulation** *and* **anguish**, upon every soul of man that *doeth* <u>evil</u>, of the Jew first, and also of the Gentile; But glory, honour, and peace, to *every man that worketh good*, to the Jew first, and also to the Gentile: For there is no respect of persons with God. For as many as have sinned without law shall also **PERISH** without law: and as many as have sinned in the law shall be judged by the law; (For *not <u>the hearers</u>* of the law are just before God, *but **<u>the doers</u>*** of the law shall be justified. For when the Gentiles, which have not the law, do by nature the things contained in the law, these, having not the law, are a law unto themselves: Which shew the work of the law written in their hearts, *their conscience* also bearing witness, and their thoughts the mean while accusing or else excusing one another;) **In the day when God shall judge the secrets of men by Jesus Christ** according to my gospel. (Romans 2:1-16)

For the preaching of the cross is to them that PERISH foolishness; but unto us which are saved it is the power of God. (1 Corinthians 1:18)

For we are unto God a sweet savour of Christ, in them that are saved, and **in them that PERISH**: To the one we are the **savour of death unto death**; and to the other the savour of *life unto life*. And who is sufficient for these things? (2 Corinthians 2:15-16)

And then shall that Wicked be revealed, whom the Lord shall consume with the spirit of his mouth, and shall destroy with the brightness of his coming: Even him, whose coming is after the working of **Satan** with all power and signs and lying wonders, And with *all deceivableness* of unrighteousness in them that **PERISH**; because they received *not* the love of the truth, that they might be saved. And for this cause **God shall send them strong delusion, that they should believe a lie: That they all might be damned** who believed not the truth, but had pleasure in *un*righteousness. (2 Thessalonians 2:8-12)

Let the brother of low degree rejoice in that he is exalted: **But the rich,** in that he is made low: because as the flower of the grass he shall pass away. For the sun is no sooner risen with a burning heat, but it withereth the grass, and the flower thereof falleth, and the grace of the fashion of it **PERISHETH: so also shall the rich man fade away in his ways.** (James 1:9-11)

But these, **as natural brute beasts, made to be taken and destroyed,** speak evil of the things that they understand not; and **shall utterly PERISH in their own corruption;** And shall receive the reward of *un*righteousness, as they that count it pleasure to riot in the day time. Spots they are and blemishes, sporting themselves with **their own deceivings** while they feast with you; Having eyes full of adultery, and that **cannot cease from sin**; beguiling unstable souls: an heart they have exercised with covetous practices; cursed children: Which have forsaken the right way, and are gone astray, following the way of Balaam the son of Bosor, who loved the wages of *un*righteousness; But was rebuked for his iniquity: the dumb ass speaking with man's voice forbad the madness of the prophet. These are wells without water, clouds that are carried with a tempest; **to whom the mist of darkness is reserved for ever.** For when they speak great swelling words of vanity, they allure through the lusts of the flesh, through much wantonness, those that were clean escaped from them who live in error. While they promise them liberty, they themselves are the **servants of corruption:** for of whom a man is overcome, of the same is he brought in bondage. For if after they have escaped the pollutions of the world through the knowledge of the Lord and Saviour Jesus Christ, they are **again entangled** therein, and **overcome,** the latter end is worse with them than the beginning. For it had been <u>better for them not to have known the way of righteousness, than, after they have known it, to turn from the holy commandment delivered unto them</u>. But it is happened unto them according to the true proverb, **The dog is turned to his own vomit again; and the sow that was washed to her wallowing in the mire.** (2 Peter 2:12-22)

But these <u>speak evil of those things which they know not</u>: but what they know naturally, as brute beasts, in those things **they corrupt themselves.** Woe unto them! for they have gone in the way of Cain, and ran greedily after the error of Balaam for reward, and **PERISHED** in the gainsaying of Core. These are spots in your feasts of charity, when they feast with you, feeding themselves without fear: clouds they are without water, carried about of winds; trees whose fruit withereth, without fruit, twice dead, plucked up by the roots; Raging waves of the sea, foaming out their own shame; wandering stars, **to whom is reserved the blackness of darkness for ever.** And Enoch also, the seventh from Adam, prophesied of these, saying, Behold, the Lord cometh with ten thousands of his saints, To execute judgment upon all, and to convince all that are ungodly among them of all their ungodly deeds which they have ungodly committed, and of all their hard speeches which ungodly sinners have spoken against him. These are <u>murmurers, complainers, walking after their own lusts</u>; and their <u>mouth speaketh great swelling words</u>, having men's persons in admiration because of advantage. But, beloved, remember ye the words which were spoken before of the apostles of our Lord Jesus

Christ; How that **they told you there should be mockers in the last time, who should walk (live) after their own ungodly lusts. These be they who <u>separate</u> <u>*themselves*</u>, sensual, having not the Spirit.** (Jude 1:10-19)

Chapter 18

GUILTY

As it is written, There is <u>none</u> righteous, no, <u>not one</u>: There is <u>none</u> that understandeth, there is **none that seeketh after God**. They are all gone out of the way, <u>they are together become unprofitable</u>; there is <u>none</u> that doeth good, no, not one. Their <u>throat is an open sepulchre</u>; with <u>their tongues they have used deceit</u>; <u>the poison of asps is under their lips</u>: <u>Whose mouth is full of cursing and bitterness</u>: <u>Their feet are swift to shed blood</u>: **Destruction and misery are in their ways:** And the way of peace have they not known: *There is no fear of God before their eyes.* Now we know that what things soever *the law* saith, it saith to them who are under the law: **that every mouth may be stopped, and all the world may become GUILTY before God.** Therefore by the deeds of the law there shall no flesh be justified in his sight: *for by the law is the knowledge of sin.* (Romans 3:10-20)

For I have received of the Lord that which also I delivered unto you, that the Lord Jesus the same night in which he was betrayed took bread: And when he had given thanks, he brake it, and said, Take, eat: this is my body, which is broken for you: this do in remembrance of me. After the same manner also he took the cup, when he had supped, saying, this cup is the new testament in my blood:

this do ye, as oft as ye drink it, in remembrance of me. For as often as ye eat this bread, and drink this cup, ye do shew the Lord's death till he come. **Wherefore whosoever shall eat this bread, and drink this cup of the Lord, _unworthily_, shall be GUILTY of the body and blood of the Lord.** But *let a man examine himself,* and so let him eat of that bread, and drink of that cup. **For he that eateth and drinketh unworthily, eateth and drinketh** *damnation* **to himself, not discerning the Lord's body.** For this cause many are weak and sickly among you, and many sleep. For *if we would judge ourselves, we should not be judged.* But when we are judged, we are chastened of the Lord, that we should not be condemned with the world. (1 Corinthians 11:23-32)

My brethren, **have not the faith** of our Lord Jesus Christ, the Lord of glory, **with respect of persons.** For if there come unto your assembly a man with a gold ring, in goodly apparel, and there come in also a poor man in vile raiment; And ye have respect to him that weareth the gay clothing, and say unto him, Sit thou here in a good place; and say to the poor, Stand thou there, or sit here under my footstool: **Are ye not then partial in yourselves, and are become judges of evil thoughts?** Hearken, my beloved brethren, *Hath not God chosen the poor of this world rich in faith, and heirs of the kingdom which he hath promised to them that love him?* **But ye have despised the poor.** Do not rich men oppress you, and draw you before the judgment seats? Do not they blaspheme that worthy name by the which ye are called? If ye fulfil the royal law according to the scripture, *Thou shalt love thy neighbour as thyself, ye do well:* But if ye have <u>respect to persons, ye commit sin</u>, and are convinced of the law as transgressors. **For whosoever shall keep the whole law, and <u>yet offend in one point</u>, he is GUILTY of all.** For he that said, <u>Do not commit adultery</u>, said also, <u>Do not kill</u>. Now if thou commit no adultery, yet if thou kill, thou art become a transgressor of the law. So speak ye, and so do, as they that shall be judged by the law of liberty. (James 2:1-12)

Chapter 19

PUNISHMENT

Then shall he say also unto them on **the left hand, Depart from me, ye cursed, into everlasting fire, prepared for the devil and his angels:** For I was an <u>hungred</u>, and ye gave me no meat: I was <u>thirsty</u>, and ye gave me no drink: I was a <u>stranger</u>, and ye took me not in: <u>naked</u>, and ye clothed me not: <u>sick</u>, and <u>in prison</u>, and ye visited me not. Then shall they also answer him, saying, Lord, when saw we thee an hungred, or athirst, or a stranger, or naked, or sick, or in prison, and did not minister unto thee? Then shall he answer them, saying, Verily I say unto you, **Inasmuch as ye did it *not* to one of the least of these, ye did it not to me. And these shall go away into everlasting PUNISHMENT:** *but the righteous into life eternal.* (Matthew 25:41-46)

So that we ourselves glory in you in the churches of God for *your patience and faith in all your persecutions and tribulations that ye endure:* Which is <u>*a manifest token of the righteous judgment of God*</u>, *that ye may be counted worthy of the kingdom of God, for which ye also suffer:* Seeing it is a righteous thing with God to recompense tribulation to them that trouble you; And to you who are troubled rest with us, when the Lord Jesus shall be revealed from heaven with his mighty angels, **In flaming fire taking *vengeance* on them that <u>know</u>**

PUNISHMENT / 109

not God, and that obey not the gospel of our Lord Jesus Christ: Who shall be PUNISHED with everlasting destruction *from the presence of the Lord,* **and from the glory of his power;** (2 Thessalonians 1:4-9)

For **if we sin** *wilfully after* **that we have received** *the knowledge of the truth,* **there remaineth no more sacrifice for sins, But a certain fearful looking for of judgment and fiery indignation, which shall devour the adversaries.** He that despised Moses' law died without mercy under two or three witnesses: **Of how much sorer PUNISHMENT, suppose ye, shall he be thought worthy, who hath trodden under foot the Son of God, and hath counted the blood of the covenant, wherewith he was sanctified, an unholy thing, and hath done despite unto the Spirit of grace?** For we know him that hath said, **Vengeance belongeth unto me, I will recompense,** saith the Lord. And again, The Lord shall judge his people. **It is a fearful thing to fall into the hands of the living God.** (Hebrews 10:26-31)

The Lord knoweth how to deliver the godly out of temptations, and **to reserve the unjust unto the of judgment to be PUNISHED:** (2 Peter 2:9)

Chapter 20

VENGEANCE

And ye shall be betrayed both by parents, and brethren, and kinsfolks, and friends; and some of you shall they cause to be put to death. And *ye shall be hated of all men for my name's sake.* But there shall not an hair of your head perish. *In your patience possess ye your souls.* And when ye shall see Jerusalem compassed with armies, then know that the desolation thereof is nigh. Then let them which are in Judaea flee to the mountains; and let them which are in the midst of it depart out; and let not them that are in the countries enter thereinto. **For these be the days of VENGEANCE**, that all things which are written may be fulfilled. (Luke 21:16-22)

But if our unrighteousness commend the righteousness of God, what shall we say? **Is God unrighteous who taketh VENGEANCE?** (I speak as a man) ***God forbid***: for then how shall God judge the world? (Romans 3:5-6)

Recompense to no man evil for evil. Provide things honest in the sight of all men. If it be possible, as much as lieth in you, live peaceably with all men. Dearly beloved, *avenge not yourselves,* but rather give place unto wrath: for it is written, **VENGEANCE is mine; I will repay, saith the Lord.** Therefore if thine **enemy** hunger, *feed him;* if he thirst, *give him drink:* for in so doing thou shalt heap coals of fire on his head. Be not overcome of evil, but *overcome evil with good.* (Romans 12:17-21)

Seeing it is a righteous thing with God to recompense tribulation to them that trouble you; And to you who are troubled rest with us, when the Lord Jesus shall be revealed from heaven with his mighty angels, **In flaming fire taking VENGEANCE on them that *know not* God, and that *obey not* the gospel of our Lord Jesus Christ: Who shall be punished with everlasting destruction** from the presence of the Lord, and from the glory of his power; (2 Thessalonians 1:6-9)

For **if we sin _wilfully_ _after_ that we have received the knowledge of the truth, there remaineth no more sacrifice for sins, But a certain fearful looking for of judgment and fiery indignation, which shall devour the adversaries.** He that despised Moses' law died without mercy under two or three witnesses: **Of how much sorer punishment, suppose ye, shall he be thought worthy, who hath trodden under foot the Son of God, and hath counted the blood of the covenant, wherewith he was sanctified, an unholy thing, and hath done despite unto the Spirit of grace?** For we know him that hath said, **VENGEANCE belongeth unto me,** *I will recompense,* saith the Lord. And again, **The Lord shall judge his people.** *It is a fearful thing to fall*

into the hands of the living God. (Hebrews 10:26-31)

And the angels which kept not their first estate, but left their own habitation, he hath reserved in everlasting chains under darkness unto the judgment of the great day. Even as Sodom and Gomorrha, and the cities about them in like manner, giving themselves over to fornication, and going after strange flesh, **are set forth for** *an example,* **suffering the VENGEANCE of eternal fire.** (Jude 1:6-7)

Chapter 21

FIRE

Bring forth therefore fruits meet for repentance: And think not to say within yourselves, We have Abraham to our father: for I say unto you, that God is able of these stones to raise up children unto Abraham. **And now also the axe is laid unto the root of the trees: therefore every tree which bringeth not forth good fruit is hewn down, and cast into the FIRE.** I indeed baptize you with water unto repentance. but he that cometh after me is mightier than I, whose shoes I am not worthy to bear: he shall baptize you with the Holy Ghost, and with *fire*: Whose fan is in his hand, and he will throughly purge his floor, and gather his <u>*wheat*</u> into the garner; but **he will burn up the <u>chaff</u> with unquenchable FIRE.** (Matthew 3:8-12)

Ye have heard that it was said of them of old time, <u>Thou shalt not kill</u>; and whosoever shall kill shall be in danger of the judgment: But I say unto you, That whosoever is <u>angry with his brother without a cause</u> shall be in danger of the judgment: and whosoever shall say to his brother, <u>Raca</u>, shall be in danger of the council: but whosoever shall say, <u>Thou fool</u>, shall be in **danger of hell FIRE.** Therefore if thou bring thy gift to the altar, and there rememberest that thy brother hath ought against thee; Leave there thy gift before the altar, and go thy way; first be reconciled to thy brother, and then come and offer thy gift. (Matthew 5:21-24)

Even so every good tree bringeth forth good fruit; but <u>a corrupt tree bringeth forth evil fruit</u>. A good tree cannot bring forth evil fruit, neither can a corrupt tree bring forth good fruit. **Every tree that bringeth not forth good fruit is hewn down, and cast into the FIRE.** *Wherefore by their fruits ye shall know them.* **Not every one that saith unto me, Lord, Lord, shall enter into the kingdom of heaven;** but he that *doeth* the will of my Father which is in heaven. (Matthew 7:17-21)

He answered and said unto them, He that soweth the good seed is the Son of man; The field is the world; *the **good seed*** *are the children of the kingdom; but* <u>the **tares** are the children of the wicked one</u>; The enemy that sowed them is the devil; the harvest is the end of the world; and the reapers are the angels. **As therefore the <u>tares</u> are gathered and burned in the FIRE**; so shall it be in the end of this world. The Son of man shall send forth his angels, and they shall gather out of his kingdom **all things that offend, and them which do iniquity; And shall cast them into a furnace of FIRE:** there shall be wailing and gnashing of teeth. Then shall the righteous shine forth as the sun in the kingdom of their Father. *Who hath ears to hear, let him hear.* (Matthew 13:37-43)

Again, the kingdom of heaven is like unto *a net,* that was cast into the sea, and <u>gathered of every kind</u>: Which, when it was full, they drew to shore, and sat down, and gathered the good into vessels, but cast the bad away. So shall it be at the end of the world: **the angels shall come forth, and sever the <u>wicked</u> from among the <u>*just*</u>, And shall cast them into the furnace of FIRE:** there shall be wailing and gnashing of teeth. Jesus saith unto them, <u>Have ye understood all these things</u>? They say unto him, Yea, Lord. (Matthew 13:47-51)

At the same time came the disciples unto Jesus, saying, *Who is the greatest in the kingdom of heaven?* And Jesus called a little child unto him, and set him in the midst of them, And said, Verily I say unto you, Except ye be *converted*, and become as little children, ye shall not enter into the kingdom of heaven. Whosoever therefore shall *humble himself* as this little child, the same is greatest in the kingdom of heaven. And whoso shall receive one such little child in my name receiveth me. <u>**But whoso shall offend one of these little ones which believe in me, it were better for him that a millstone were hanged about his neck, and that he were drowned in the depth of the sea.**</u> *Woe* unto the world because of offences! for it must needs be that offences come; but *woe* to that man by whom the offence cometh! Wherefore <u>if thy **hand** or thy **foot** offend thee</u>, *cut them off,* and cast them from thee: **it is better for thee to enter into life halt or maimed, rather than having two hands or two feet to be cast into everlasting FIRE.** And <u>if thine *eye* offend thee</u>, *pluck it out,* and cast it from thee: **it is better for thee to enter into life with one eye, rather than having two eyes to be cast into hell FIRE.** (Matthew 18:1-9)

Then shall he say also unto them on the **left hand, Depart from me,** *ye cursed,* **into everlasting FIRE, prepared for the devil and his angels:** For I was an hungred, and ye gave me no meat: I was thirsty, and ye gave me no drink: I was a stranger, and ye took me not in: naked, and ye clothed me not: sick, and in prison, and ye visited me not. Then shall they also answer him, saying, Lord, when saw we thee an hungred, or athirst, or a stranger, or naked, or sick, or in prison, and did not minister unto thee? Then shall he answer them, saying, Verily I say unto you, **Inasmuch as ye did it not to one of the least of these, ye did it not to me. And these shall go away into everlasting punishment:** but the righteous into life eternal. (Matthew 25:41-46)

And whosoever shall **offend** one of these little ones that believe in me, **it is better for him that a millstone were hanged about his neck, and he were cast into the sea.** And if thy **hand** offend thee, *cut it off:* it is better for thee to enter into life maimed, than having two hands to go into hell, into **the FIRE that never shall be quenched: Where their worm dieth not, and the FIRE is not quenched.** And if thy **foot** offend thee, *cut it off:* it is better for thee to enter halt into life, than having two feet to be cast into hell, into **the FIRE that never shall be quenched: Where their worm dieth not, and the FIRE is not quenched.** And if thine **eye** offend thee, *pluck it out:* it is better for thee to enter into the kingdom of God with one eye, than having two eyes to be cast into **hell FIRE: Where their worm dieth not, and the fire is not quenched.** For every one shall be salted with **FIRE,** and every sacrifice shall be salted with salt. Salt is good: but <u>if the salt have lost his saltness</u>, wherewith will ye season it? Have salt in yourselves, and have peace one with another. (Mark 9:42-50)

Then said he to the multitude that came forth to be baptized of him, **O generation of vipers,** who hath warned you to flee from the wrath to come? *Bring forth therefore fruits worthy of repentance,* and begin not to say within yourselves, We have Abraham to our father: for I say unto you, That God is able of these stones to raise up children unto Abraham. And now also the axe is laid unto the root of the trees: **every tree therefore which bringeth not forth good fruit is hewn down, and cast into the FIRE.** (Luke 3:7-9)

And as the people were in expectation, and all men mused in their hearts of John, whether he were the Christ, or not; John answered, saying unto them all, I indeed baptize you with water; but one mightier than I cometh, the latchet of whose shoes I am not worthy to unloose: he shall baptize you with the Holy Ghost and with **FIRE**: Whose fan is in his hand, and *he will throughly purge his floor,* and will gather the ***wheat*** into his garner; *but* **the chaff he will burn with FIRE unquenchable.** (Luke 3:15-17)

But and if that servant say *in his heart*, <u>My lord delayeth his coming</u>; and shall begin to <u>beat the menservants and maidens</u>, and to <u>eat and drink</u>, and <u>to be drunken</u>; The lord of that servant will come in a day when he looketh not for him, and at an hour **when he is not aware, and will cut him in sunder,** and will appoint him his portion with the unbelievers. And that servant, **which _knew_ his lord's will, _and_ prepared not himself, _neither_ did according to his will, shall be beaten with many stripes.** But he that knew not, and did commit things worthy of stripes, shall be beaten with few stripes. *For unto whomsoever much is given, of him shall be much required: and to whom men have committed much, of him they will ask the more.* I am come to send **FIRE** on the earth; and what will I, if it be already kindled? But I have a baptism to be baptized with; and how am I straitened till it be accomplished! Suppose ye that I am come to give peace on earth? I tell you, **Nay; but rather division:** For from henceforth there shall be five in one house divided, three against two, and two against three. The father shall be divided against the son, and the son against the father; the mother against the daughter, and the daughter against the mother; the mother in law against her daughter in law, and the daughter in law against her mother in law. (Luke 12:45-53)

And as it was in the days of Noe, so shall it be also in the days of the Son of man. They did eat, they drank, they married wives, they were given in marriage, until the day that Noah entered into the ark, and **the flood came, *and* destroyed them all.** Likewise also as it was in the days of Lot; they did eat, they drank, they bought, they sold, they planted, they builded; But the same day that Lot went out of Sodom it rained **FIRE *and* brimstone from heaven, and destroyed them all.** Even thus shall it be in the day when the Son of man is revealed. In that day, he which shall be upon the housetop, and his stuff in the house, let him not come down to take it away: and he that is in the field, let him likewise not return back. Remember Lot's wife. **Whosoever shall seek to <u>save</u> his life shall lose it;** *and whosoever shall <u>lose</u> his life shall preserve it.* I tell you, in that night there shall be two men in one bed; the one shall be taken, and the other shall be left. Two women shall be grinding together; the one shall be taken, and the other left. Two men shall be in the field; the one shall be taken, and the other left. And they answered and said unto him, Where, Lord? And he said unto them, <u>Wheresoever the body is, thither will the eagles be gathered together</u>. (Luke 17:26-37)

If a man abide *not* in me, he is cast forth as a branch, and is withered; and men gather them, and **cast them into the FIRE, and they are burned.** (John 15:6)

But this is that which was spoken by *the prophet Joel*; And it shall come to pass in the last days, saith God, I will pour out of my Spirit upon all flesh: and your sons and your daughters shall prophesy, and your young men shall see visions, and your old men shall dream dreams: *And on my servants and on my handmaidens I will pour out in those days of my Spirit;* and they shall prophesy: And I will shew wonders in heaven above, and signs in the earth beneath; **blood, and FIRE, and vapour of smoke:** <u>The sun shall be turned into darkness, and the moon into blood</u>, *before the great and notable day of the Lord come:* And it shall come to pass, that whosoever shall call on the name of the Lord shall be saved. (Acts 2:16-21)

Dearly beloved, avenge not yourselves, but rather give place unto wrath: for it is written, *Vengeance is mine; I will repay, saith the Lord.* Therefore if thine enemy hunger, <u>feed him</u>; if he thirst, <u>give him drink</u>: for in so doing thou shalt heap coals of **FIRE** on his head. **Be not overcome of evil,** *but overcome evil with good.* (Romans 12:19-21)

<u>Every man's work shall be made manifest</u>: for the day shall declare it, because it shall be revealed by **FIRE**; and **the FIRE shall** *try* **every man's work of what sort it is.** If any man's work *abide* which he hath built thereupon, he shall receive a *reward*. If any man's work shall be <u>burned</u>, he shall suffer <u>loss</u>: but he himself shall be saved; yet so as by **FIRE.** (1 Corinthians 3:13-15)

We are bound to thank God always for you, brethren, as it is meet, because that your faith groweth exceedingly, and *the charity of every one of you all toward each other aboundeth;* So that we ourselves glory in you in the churches of God for *your patience and faith in all your persecutions and tribulations that ye endure:* Which is a manifest token of the righteous judgment of God, *that ye may be counted worthy of the kingdom of God,* for which ye also suffer: Seeing it is a righteous thing with God to recompense tribulation to them that trouble you; And to you who are troubled rest with us, when the Lord Jesus shall be revealed from heaven with his mighty angels. In flaming **FIRE**

taking vengeance on them that *know not* God, and that *obey not* the gospel of our Lord Jesus Christ: Who shall be punished with everlasting destruction from the presence of the Lord, and from the glory of his power; (2 Thessalonians 1:3-9)

For ye are not come unto the mount that might be touched, and that burned with **FIRE**, nor unto blackness, and darkness, and tempest, And the sound of a trumpet, and the voice of words; which voice they that heard intreated that the word should not be spoken to them any more: (For they could not endure that which was commanded, And if so much as a beast touch the mountain, it shall be stoned, or thrust through with a dart: **And so terrible was the sight, that Moses said, I exceedingly fear and quake:**) But ye are come unto mount Sion, and unto the city of the living God, the heavenly Jerusalem, and to an innumerable company of angels, To the general assembly and church of the firstborn, which are written in heaven, and to God the Judge of all, and to the spirits of just men made perfect, And to Jesus the mediator of the new covenant, and to the blood of sprinkling, that speaketh better things than that of Abel. See that ye refuse not him that speaketh. <u>For if they escaped not who refused him that spake on earth, much more shall not we escape, if we turn away from him that speaketh from heaven</u>: Whose voice then shook the earth: but now he hath promised, saying, **Yet once more I shake not the earth only, but *also* heaven.** And this word, Yet once more, signifieth the removing of those things that are shaken, as of things that are made, that those things which cannot be shaken may remain. Wherefore we receiving a kingdom which cannot be moved, let us have grace, whereby *we may serve God acceptably with reverence and godly fear: For our God is a consuming* **FIRE**. (Hebrews 12:18)

Even so **the tongue** is a little member, and boasteth great things. Behold, how great a matter a little **FIRE** kindleth! And **the tongue is a FIRE, a world of iniquity:** so is the tongue among our members, that it defileth the whole body, and setteth on fire the course of nature; and **it is set on fire of hell.** (James 3:5-6)

Go to now, **ye rich men,** weep and howl for your miseries that shall come upon you. Your riches are corrupted, and your garments are motheaten. Your gold and silver is cankered; and the rust of them shall be a witness against you, and shall eat your flesh as it were **FIRE**. Ye have heaped treasure together for the last days. Behold, the hire of the labourers who have reaped down your fields, which is of you kept back by fraud, crieth: and the cries of them which have reaped are entered into the ears of the Lord of sabaoth. Ye have lived in pleasure on the earth, and been wanton; ye have nourished your hearts, as in a day of slaughter. Ye have condemned and killed the just; and he doth not resist you. (James 5:1-6)

Wherein ye greatly rejoice, though now for a season, if need be, ye are in heaviness through manifold temptations: That *the trial of your faith,* being much more precious than of gold that perisheth, though it be *tried with* **FIRE**, might be found unto praise and honour and glory at the appearing of Jesus Christ: (1 Peter 1:6-7)

That ye may be mindful of the words which were spoken before by the holy prophets, and of the commandment of us the apostles of the Lord and Saviour: Knowing this first, that there shall come **in the last days scoffers, walking after their own lusts**, And saying, Where is the promise of his coming? for since the fathers fell asleep, all things continue as they were from the beginning of the creation. For this they willingly are ignorant of, that by the word of God the heavens were of old, and the earth standing out of the water and in the water: Whereby the world that then was, being overflowed with water, perished: But the heavens and the earth, which are now, by the same word are kept in store, **reserved unto FIRE against the day of judgment and perdition of *ungodly* men.** (2 Peter 3:2-7)

But, beloved, be not ignorant of this one thing, that one day is with the Lord as a thousand years, and a thousand years as one day. The Lord is not slack concerning his promise, as some men count slackness; but is longsuffering to us-ward, *not willing that any should perish, but that all should come to repentance.* But the day of the Lord will come as a thief in the night; in the which the heavens shall pass away with a great noise, and the elements shall melt with fervent heat, the earth also and the works that are therein shall be burned up. Seeing then that all these things shall be dissolved, **what manner of persons ought ye to be in all holy** *conversation and godliness,* Looking for and hasting unto the coming of the day of God, wherein the heavens being on **FIRE** shall be dissolved, and the elements shall melt with fervent heat? (2 Peter 3:8-12)

Beloved, when I gave all diligence to write unto you of the common salvation, it was needful for me to write unto you, and exhort you that ye should *earnestly contend for the faith* which was once delivered unto the saints. For there are certain men crept in unawares, who were before of old ordained to this condemnation, **ungodly men, turning the grace of our God into lasciviousness**, and denying the only Lord God, and our Lord Jesus Christ. I will therefore put you in remembrance, though ye once knew this, how that the Lord, having saved the people out of the land of Egypt, afterward destroyed them that believed not. And the angels which kept not their first estate, but left their own habitation, he hath reserved in everlasting chains under darkness unto the judgment of the great day. Even as Sodom and Gomorrha, and the cities about them in like manner, giving themselves over to fornication, and going after strange flesh, **are set forth for an example, suffering the vengeance of eternal FIRE**. (Jude 1:3-7)

Keep yourselves in the love of God, looking for the mercy of our Lord Jesus Christ unto eternal life. And of some have compassion, making a difference: And others save with fear, pulling them out of the **FIRE**; hating even the garment spotted by the flesh. (Jude 1:21-23)

And in the midst of the <u>seven candlesticks</u> one *like unto the Son of man*, clothed with a garment down to the foot, and girt about the paps with a golden girdle. His head and his hairs were white like wool, as white as snow; and ***his eyes were as a flame of* FIRE**; And his feet like unto fine brass, as if they burned in a furnace; and his voice as the sound of many waters. (Revelation 1:13-15)

And unto the angel of the <u>church in Thyatira</u> write; *These things saith the Son of God,* who hath his eyes like unto a flame of **FIRE**, and his feet are like fine brass; I know thy works, and charity, and service, and faith, and thy patience, and thy works; and the last to be more than the first. *Notwithstanding I have a few things against thee, because* **thou sufferest that woman Jezebel, which** *calleth* **herself a prophetess, to teach and to seduce my servants to commit fornication, and to eat things sacrificed unto idols.** And *I gave her space to repent of her fornication;* and **she repented not.** Behold, I will cast her into a bed, and them that commit <u>adultery</u> with her into great tribulation, except they *repent of their deeds.* And I will kill her children with death; and all the churches shall know that ***I am he which searcheth the reins and hearts:*** and ***I will give unto every one of you according to your works.*** But unto you I say, and unto the rest in Thyatira, as many as have not this doctrine, and which have not known the depths of Satan, as they speak; I will put upon you none other burden. But that which ye have already hold fast till I come. And he that ***overcometh, and keepeth my works unto the end,*** to him will I give power over the nations: And he shall rule them with a rod of iron; as the vessels of a potter shall they be broken to shivers: even as I received of my Father. And I will give him the morning star. *He that hath an ear, let him hear* what the Spirit saith unto the churches. (Revelation 2:18)

And unto the angel of the <u>church of the Laodiceans</u> write; These things saith the Amen, the faithful and true witness, the beginning of the creation of God; *I know thy works, that* **thou art neither cold nor hot: I would thou wert cold or hot. So then because thou art <u>lukewarm</u>, and neither cold nor hot,** *I will spue thee out of my mouth.* Because thou sayest, <u>I am rich</u>, and <u>increased with goods</u>, and <u>have need of nothing</u>; and <u>knowest **not** that thou art wretched</u>, and <u>miserable</u>, and <u>poor</u>, and <u>blind</u>, and <u>naked</u>: *I counsel thee to buy of me gold tried in the* **FIRE**, that thou mayest be rich; and white raiment, that thou mayest be clothed, and that the shame of thy nakedness do not appear; and anoint thine eyes with eyesalve, that thou mayest see. ***As many as I love, I rebuke and chasten: be zealous therefore, and <u>repent</u>.*** Behold, I stand at the door, and knock: if any man hear my voice, and open the door, I will come in to him, and will sup with him, and he with me. To him that ***overcometh*** will I grant to sit with me in my throne, <u>*even as I also overcame*</u>, and am set down with my Father in his throne. *He that hath an ear, let him hear* what the Spirit saith unto the churches. (Revelation 3:14-22)

And the _seven angels_ which had the _seven trumpets_ prepared themselves to sound. The _first angel_ sounded, and there followed hail and **FIRE** mingled with blood, and they were cast upon the earth: and the third part of trees was burnt up, and all green grass was burnt up. And the _second angel_ sounded, and as it were *a great mountain burning with* **FIRE** was cast into the sea: and the third part of the sea became blood; And the third part of the creatures which were in the sea, and had life, died; and the third part of the ships were destroyed. And the _third angel_ sounded, and there fell a great star from heaven, burning as it were a lamp, and it fell upon the third part of the rivers, and upon the fountains of waters; And the name of the star is called **Wormwood**: and the third part of the waters became wormwood; and many men died of the waters, because they were made bitter. And the _fourth angel_ sounded, and the third part of the sun was smitten, and the third part of the moon, and the third part of the stars; so as the third part of them was darkened, and the day shone not for a third part of it, and the night likewise. And I behold, and heard an angel flying through the midst of heaven, saying with a loud voice, **Woe, woe, woe, to the inhabiters of the earth** by reason of the other voices of the trumpet of the three angels, which are yet to sound! (Revelation 8:6-13)

And the _sixth angel_ sounded, and *I heard a voice from the four horns of the* **golden altar** *which is before God,* Saying to the sixth angel which had the trumpet, Loose the four angels which are bound in the great river Euphrates. And *the four angels* *were loosed*, which were prepared for an hour, and a day, and a month, and a year, for to slay the third part of men. And the number of the army of the horsemen were two hundred thousand thousand: and I heard the number of them. And thus I saw the **horses** in the vision, and them that sat on them, having breastplates of fire, and of jacinth, and brimstone: and the heads of the horses were as the heads of lions; and out of their mouths issued **FIRE** and smoke and brimstone. By these three was the third part of men killed, by the **FIRE**, and by the smoke, and by the brimstone, which issued out of their mouths. For their power is in their mouth, and in their tails: for their tails were like unto serpents, and had heads, and with them they do hurt. And **the rest of the men which were not killed by these plagues** *yet repented not* **of the works of their hands, that they should not worship devils, and idols** of gold, and silver, and brass, and stone, and of wood: which neither can see, nor hear, nor walk: **Neither repented they** of their murders, nor of their sorceries, nor of their fornication, nor of their thefts. (Revelation 9:13-21)

And I saw *another mighty angel* come down from heaven, clothed with a cloud: and a rainbow was upon his head, and his face was as it were the sun, and his feet as pillars of **FIRE**: And he had in his hand *a little book open*: and he set his right foot upon the sea, and his left foot on the earth, And *cried with a loud voice,* as when a lion roareth: and when he had cried, seven thunders uttered their voices. And when the seven thunders had uttered their voices, I was about to write: and I heard a voice from heaven saying unto me, Seal up those things which the seven thunders uttered, and write them not. And the angel which I saw stand upon the sea and upon the earth lifted up his hand to heaven, And <u>sware by him that liveth for ever and ever</u>, who created heaven, and the things that therein are, and the earth, and the things that therein are, and the sea, and the things which are therein, that *there should be time no longer:* But in the days of the voice of the <u>seventh angel</u>, when he shall begin to sound, the mystery of God should be finished, as he hath declared to his servants the prophets. And the voice which I heard from heaven spake unto me again, and said, Go and take *the little book* which is open in the hand of the angel which standeth upon the sea and upon the earth. And I went unto the angel, and said unto him, Give me *the little book.* And he said unto me, <u>Take it, and eat it up; and it shall make thy belly bitter, but it shall be in thy mouth sweet as honey</u>. And I took *the little book* out of the angel's hand, and ate it up; and it was in my mouth sweet as honey: and as soon as I had eaten it, my belly was bitter. And he said unto me, *Thou must prophesy again before many peoples, and nations, and tongues, and kings.* (Revelation 10:1-11)

And there was given me a reed like unto a rod: and the angel stood, saying, *Rise, and measure the temple of God, and the altar, and them that worship therein.* But the <u>court which is without</u> the temple leave out, and <u>measure it not</u>; for it is given unto the <u>Gentiles</u>: and the holy city shall they tread under <u>foot forty and two months</u>. And I will give power unto *my two witnesses*, and they shall prophesy a thousand two hundred and threescore days, clothed in sackcloth. These are the *two olive trees*, and the *two candlesticks* standing before the God of the earth. And if any man will hurt them, **FIRE** *proceedeth out of their mouth, and devoureth their enemies:* and if any man will hurt them, he must in this manner be killed. These have power to shut heaven, that it rain not in the days of their prophecy: and have power over waters to turn them to blood, and to smite the earth with all plagues, as often as they will. And when they shall have finished their testimony, the beast that ascendeth out of the bottomless pit shall make war against them, and shall overcome them, and kill them. And their dead bodies shall lie in the street of **the great city,** which *spiritually is called* Sodom and Egypt, where also our Lord was crucified. And they of the people and kindreds and tongues and nations shall see their dead bodies three days and an half, and shall not suffer their dead bodies to be put in graves. And they that dwell upon the earth shall rejoice over them, and make merry, and shall send gifts one to another; because **these two prophets tormented them that dwelt on the earth.** *And after three days and an half the spirit of life from God entered into them, and they stood upon their feet;* and great fear fell upon them which saw them. (Revelation 11:1-11)

And I beheld *another* beast coming up out of the earth; and he had two horns like a lamb, and he spake as a dragon. And he exerciseth all the power of the first beast before him, and causeth the earth and them which dwell therein to **worship the first**

beast, whose deadly wound was healed. And he doeth great wonders, so that he maketh **FIRE** come down from heaven on the earth in the sight of men, And **deceiveth them** that dwell on the earth by the means of those miracles which he had power to do in the sight of the beast; saying to them that dwell on the earth, that they should make an image to the beast, which had the wound by a sword, and did live. And he had power to give life unto the image of the beast, that the image of the beast should both speak, and cause **that as many as would not worship the image of the beast should be killed**. And he causeth all, both small and great, rich and poor, free and bond, to receive **a mark** in their right hand, *or* in their foreheads: And that no man might buy or sell, save he that had **the mark**, *or* the name of the beast, *or* the number of his name. Here is wisdom. Let him that hath understanding count the number of the beast: for it is the number of a man; and his number is Six hundred threescore and six. (Revelation 13:11-17)

And there followed *another angel*, saying, **Babylon is fallen, is fallen, that great city, because she made all nations drink of the wine of the wrath of her fornication.** And the *third angel* followed them, saying with a loud voice, *If any man worship the beast and his image, and receive his mark in his forehead, or in his hand, The same shall drink of the wine of the wrath of God,* which is poured out without mixture into the cup of *his indignation*; and he shall be tormented with **FIRE** and brimstone in the presence of the holy angels, and in the presence of the Lamb: And the smoke of their torment ascendeth up for ever and ever: and they have ***no rest day nor night,*** who **worship the beast** and his image, and whosoever **receiveth the mark** of his name. (Revelation 14:8-11)

And he that sat on the cloud thrust in his sickle on the earth; and *the earth was reaped.* And <u>another angel</u> came out of the temple which is in heaven, he also having a sharp sickle. And <u>*another angel*</u> came out from the altar, which had power over **FIRE**; and cried with a loud cry to him that had the sharp sickle, saying, *Thrust in thy sharp sickle, and gather the clusters of the vine of the earth; for her grapes are fully ripe.* And the angel thrust in his sickle into the earth, and gathered the vine of the earth, and **cast it into the great winepress of the wrath of God.** And the winepress was trodden without the city, and blood came out of the winepress, even unto the horse bridles, by the space of a thousand and six hundred furlongs. (Revelation 14:16-20)

And I heard a great voice out of the temple saying to the <u>seven angels</u>, ***Go your ways, and pour out the vials of the wrath of God upon the earth.*** And the <u>first</u> went, and poured out his vial upon the earth; and there fell a noisome and *grievous sore* upon the men <u>which had the mark of the beast,</u> and upon them which <u>worshipped his image</u>. And the <u>second angel</u> poured out his vial upon <u>the sea</u>; and it became as the *blood* of a dead man: and every living soul died in the sea. And the <u>third angel</u> poured out his vial upon *the rivers and fountains* of waters; and they became *blood.* And I heard the angel of the waters say, Thou art righteous, O Lord,

FIRE / 133

which art, and wast, and shalt be, because ***thou hast judged thus. For <u>they</u> have shed the blood of saints and prophets, and thou hast given <u>them</u> blood to drink; for they are worthy.*** And I heard another out of the altar say, Even so, Lord God Almighty, true and righteous are thy judgments. And the *fourth angel* poured out his vial upon the <u>sun</u>; and power was given unto him to *scorch men with* **FIRE**. And men were scorched with great heat, and blasphemed the name of God, which hath power over these plagues: and **they repented not** to give him glory. (Revelation 16:1-9)

And he saith unto me, <u>The waters</u> which thou sawest, where **the whore** sitteth, are peoples, and multitudes, and nations, and tongues. And the <u>ten horns</u> which thou sawest upon the beast, <u>these shall hate the whore</u>, and shall make her desolate and naked, and shall eat her flesh, and burn her with **FIRE**. For God hath put in their hearts to fulfil his will, and to agree, and give their kingdom unto the beast, until the words of God shall be fulfilled. **<u>And the woman which thou sawest is that great city, which reigneth over the kings of the earth.</u>** (Revelation 17:15-18)

And after these things I saw *another angel* come down from heaven, having great power; and the earth was lightened with his glory. And he cried mightily with a strong voice, saying, **Babylon the great is fallen, is fallen,** and is become the <u>habitation of devils</u>, and the hold of <u>every foul spirit</u>, and a cage of <u>every unclean and hateful bird</u>. For **all nations** have drunk of the wine of the wrath of her <u>fornication</u>, and **the kings** of the earth have <u>committed fornication with her</u>, and **the merchants** of the earth are waxed rich through the abundance of her delicacies. And I heard another voice from heaven, saying, ***Come out of her, <u>my people</u>, that ye be not partakers of her sins, and that ye receive not of her plagues.*** For her sins have reached unto heaven, and God hath remembered her iniquities. Reward her even as she rewarded you, and **double unto her double** according to her works: in the cup which she hath filled fill to her double. How much she hath <u>glorified herself</u>, and <u>lived deliciously</u>, so much torment and sorrow give her: for she saith in her heart, **I sit a queen,** and am no widow, and shall see no sorrow. Therefore shall **her plagues** come in one day, <u>death</u>, and <u>mourning</u>, and <u>famine</u>; and **she shall be utterly burned with FIRE: for strong is the Lord God who judgeth her.** And the kings of the earth, who have committed <u>fornication</u> and <u>lived deliciously</u> with her, shall bewail her, and lament for her, when they shall see the smoke of her burning, Standing afar off for the fear of her torment, saying, Alas, alas that great city **Babylon**, that mighty city! for <u>in one hour is thy judgment come</u>. And the merchants of the earth shall weep and mourn over her; for no man buyeth their merchandise any more: (Revelation 18:1-11)

And I saw heaven opened, and behold a <u>white horse</u>; and he that sat upon him was called <u>Faithful and True</u>, and *in righteousness he doth judge* and make war. His *eyes* were as a flame of **FIRE**, and *on his head were **many crowns***; and he had a name written, that no man knew, but he himself. And he was <u>clothed with a vesture dipped in blood</u>: and ***his name is called The Word of God.*** And *the armies* which were in heaven followed him upon white horses, clothed in fine linen, white and clean. And *out of his mouth goeth a sharp sword,* that with it he should <u>smite the nations</u>: and he shall rule them with a <u>rod of iron</u>: and ***he treadeth the winepress of the <u>fierceness</u> and <u>wrath</u> of Almighty God.*** And he hath on his vesture and on his thigh a name written, KING OF KINGS, AND LORD OF LORDS. And I saw <u>*an angel*</u> standing in the sun; and he cried with a loud voice, saying to all the fowls that fly in the midst of heaven, Come and gather yourselves together unto the <u>supper of the great God</u>; That ye may eat the flesh of <u>kings</u>, and the flesh of <u>captains,</u> and the flesh of <u>mighty men,</u> and the <u>flesh of horses,</u> and of them that sit on them, and the flesh of <u>all men</u>, both free and bond, both small and great. And I saw **the beast**, and **the kings** of the earth, and their **armies**, gathered together to make war against him that sat on the horse, and against his army. And **the beast** <u>was taken,</u> and with him the **false prophet** that wrought miracles before him, with which ***he deceived* them that had received the *mark* of the beast, and them that *worshipped* his image.** These <u>both were cast alive into a lake of **FIRE** burning with brimstone</u>. And the remnant were slain with the sword of him that sat upon the horse, which sword proceeded out of his mouth: and all the fowls were filled with their flesh. (Revelation 19:11-21)

And I saw *an angel* come down from heaven, having the key of the bottomless pit and a great chain in his hand. And he laid hold on the **<u>dragon</u>**, that **old serpent**, which is the **Devil**, and **Satan**, and <u>bound him a thousand years</u>, And cast him into the bottomless pit, and shut him up, and set a seal upon him, that **he should *deceive* the nations no more**, till the thousand years should be fulfilled: and after that he must be loosed a little season. And I saw *thrones,* and they sat upon them, and judgment was given unto them: and I saw the *souls of them that were <u>beheaded for the witness of Jesus, and for the word of God</u>,* and which had <u>*not worshipped the beast*</u>, neither his image, <u>neither had received his mark</u> upon their foreheads, or in their hands; and <u>they lived and reigned with Christ a thousand years</u>. But the rest of the dead lived not again until the thousand years were finished. This is the <u>*first resurrection*</u>. Blessed and holy is he that hath part in the first resurrection: on such the second death hath no power, but *they shall be <u>priests</u> of God and of Christ, and <u>shall reign with him</u> a thousand years*. And when the thousand years are expired, Satan shall be loosed out of his prison, And shall go out **to deceive the nations** which are in the four quarters of the earth, Gog, and Magog, to gather them together to battle: the number of whom is as the sand of the sea. And they went up on the breadth of the earth, and compassed the camp of the saints about, and the beloved city: and **FIRE** came down from God out of heaven, and devoured them. And **the devil** that *deceived* them was cast into the lake of **FIRE** and brimstone, where the <u>beast</u> and the <u>false prophet</u> are, and shall be tormented day and night for ever and ever. And I saw a ***great white throne,*** and him that sat on it, from whose face the earth and the heaven fled away; and there was

FIRE / 137

found no place for them. And I saw the dead, small and great, **stand before God;** and *the books were opened:* and another book was opened, which is the book of life: and the dead were judged out of those things which were written in the *books, according to their works.* And the sea gave up the dead which were in it; and death and hell delivered up the dead which were in them: and **they were judged every man according to their works.** And death and hell were cast into the lake of **FIRE**. This is the second death. And whosoever was not found written in the book of life was cast into the lake of **FIRE**. (Revelation 20:1-15)

He that **overcometh** *shall inherit all things;* and I will be his God, and he shall be my son. ***But*** the fearful, and unbelieving, and the abominable, and murderers, and whoremongers, and sorcerers, and idolaters, and *all liars,* **shall have their part in the lake which burneth with FIRE and brimstone:** which is the second death. (Revelation 21:7-8)

Chapter 22

WRATH

In those days came John the Baptist, preaching in the wilderness of Judaea, And saying, ***Repent ye:*** for the kingdom of heaven is at hand. For this is he that was spoken of by the prophet Esaias, saying, The voice of one crying in the wilderness, <u>*Prepare ye the way of the Lord, make his paths straight*</u>. And the same John had his raiment of camel's hair, and a leathern girdle about his loins; and his meat was locusts and wild honey. Then went out to him Jerusalem, and all Judaea, and all the region round about Jordan, And were baptized of him in Jordan, *confessing their sins.* But when he saw many of the Pharisees and Sadducees come to his baptism, he said unto them, <u>O generation of vipers</u>, who hath warned you to flee from the **WRATH** to come? ***Bring forth therefore fruits meet for repentance*:** (Matthew 3:1-8)

So when his fellowservants saw what was done, they were very sorry, and came and told unto their lord all that was done. Then his lord, after that he had called him, said unto him, *O thou wicked servant, I forgave thee all that debt, because thou desiredst me: Shouldest not thou also have had compassion on thy fellowservant, even as I had pity on thee?* And his lord was **WR<u>O</u>TH**, and delivered him to the tormentors, till he should pay all that was due unto him. **So likewise shall my heavenly Father do also unto you, if ye** *from your hearts* **forgive not every one his brother their trespasses.** (Matthew 18:31-35)

And Jesus answered and spake unto them again by parables, and said, The kingdom of heaven is like unto a certain king, which made a marriage for his son, And sent forth his servants to call them that were **bidden to the wedding**: and they would not come. Again, he sent forth other servants, saying, Tell them which are bidden, Behold, I have prepared my dinner: my oxen and my fatlings are killed, and all things are ready: come unto the marriage. But they made light of it, and went their ways, one to his farm, another to his merchandise: And the remnant took his servants, and entreated them spitefully, and slew them. But when the king heard thereof, he was **WROTH**: and he sent forth his armies, and destroyed those murderers, and burned up their city. Then saith he to his servants, The wedding is ready, but **they which were bidden were not worthy.** (Matthew 22:1-8)

And he (John the Baptist) came into all the country about Jordan, *preaching the **baptism of repentance** for the remission of sins;* As it is written in the book of the words of Esaias the prophet, saying, The voice of one crying in the wilderness, Prepare ye the way of the Lord, make his paths straight. Every valley shall be filled, and every mountain and hill shall be brought low; and the crooked shall be made straight, and the rough ways shall be made smooth; And all flesh shall see the salvation of God. Then said he to the multitude that came forth to be baptized of him, O generation of vipers, who hath warned you to flee from the **WRATH** to come? **Bring forth therefore fruits worthy of repentance,** and begin not to say within yourselves,

We have Abraham to our father: for I say unto you, That God is able of these stones to raise up children unto Abraham. And now also <u>the axe is laid unto the root of the trees</u>: **every tree therefore which bringeth not forth good fruit is hewn down, and cast into the fire.** (Luke 3:3-9)

And ye shall be betrayed both by parents, and brethren, and kinsfolks, and friends; and some of you shall they cause to be put to death. And *ye shall be hated of all men for my name's sake.* But there shall not an hair of your head perish. In your patience possess ye your souls. And when ye shall see Jerusalem compassed with armies, then know that the desolation thereof is nigh. Then let them which are in Judaea flee to the mountains; and let them which are in the midst of it depart out; and let not them that are in the countries enter thereinto. *For these be the days of vengeance,* that all things which are written may be fulfilled. But woe unto them that are with child, and to them that give suck, in those days! for there shall be great distress in the land, and **WRATH** upon this people. And they shall fall by the edge of the sword, and shall be led away captive into all nations: and Jerusalem shall be trodden down of the Gentiles, until the times of the Gentiles be fulfilled. (Luke 21:16-24)

He that believeth on the Son hath everlasting life: and <u>he that believeth *not* the Son</u> shall not see life; *but* **the WRATH of God abideth on him.** (John 3:36)

For the WRATH of God is revealed from heaven against all ungodliness and unrighteousness of men, who hold the truth in unrighteousness; Because that which may be known of God is manifest in them; for *God hath shewed it unto them.* For the invisible things of him from the creation of the world are clearly seen, being understood by the things that are made, even his eternal power and Godhead; so that **they are without excuse:** Because that, *when they knew God*, they <u>glorified him not as God</u>, <u>neither were thankful</u>; but became <u>vain in their imaginations</u>, and their <u>foolish heart was darkened</u>. Professing themselves to be wise, they became <u>fools</u>, And changed the glory of the uncorruptible God into an <u>image</u> made like to corruptible man, and to birds, and fourfooted beasts, and creeping things. Wherefore **God also gave them up** to <u>uncleanness through the lusts of their own hearts, to dishonour their own bodies between themselves</u>: Who **changed the truth** of God into *a lie*, and <u>worshipped and served the creature</u> more than the Creator, who is blessed for ever. Amen. For this cause **God gave them up unto vile affections:** for even their <u>women</u> did change the natural use into that which is <u>against nature</u>: And likewise also the <u>men</u>, leaving the natural use of the woman, <u>burned in their lust one toward another</u>; <u>men with men</u> working that which is unseemly, and **receiving in themselves that recompence of their error** *which was meet*. And even as <u>they did not like to retain God in their knowledge</u>, **God gave them over to a reprobate mind**, <u>to do those things which are not convenient</u>; Being filled with ***all*** <u>unrighteousness, fornication, wickedness, covetousness,</u>

maliciousness; full of envy, murder, debate, deceit, malignity; whisperers, Backbiters, haters of God, despiteful, proud, boasters, inventors of evil things, disobedient to parents, Without understanding, covenantbreakers, without natural affection, implacable, unmerciful: Who knowing the judgment of God, that they which commit such things **are worthy of death**, not only do the same, *but* **have pleasure in them** that do them. (Romans 1:1-32)

Therefore thou art *inexcusable*, O man, whosoever thou art that judgest: for wherein thou judgest another, thou condemnest thyself; for thou that judgest doest the same things. But we are sure that *the judgment of God is according to truth* against them which commit such things. And thinkest thou this, O man, that judgest them which do such things, and doest the same, that thou shalt escape the judgment of God? **Or despisest thou *the riches of his goodness and forbearance and longsuffering; not knowing that the goodness of God leadeth thee to repentance?* But after thy hardness and impenitent heart treasurest up unto thyself WRATH against the day of WRATH and revelation of the righteous judgment of God;** *Who will render to every man according to his deeds:* To them who by *patient continuance in well **doing** seek for glory and honour and immortality, eternal life*: But unto them that are contentious, and do not obey the truth, but obey **un**righteousness, **indignation and WRATH, Tribulation and anguish, upon every soul of man that *doeth* evil,** of the Jew first, and also of the Gentile; But *glory, honour*, and *peace*, to every man that <u>worketh good</u>, to the Jew first, and also to the Gentile: For there is no respect of persons with God. (Romans 2:1-11)

Because *the law worketh* **WRATH**: for where *no* law is, there is *no* transgression. (Romans 4:15)

Much more then, being now *justified by his blood*, ***we shall be saved from* WRATH *through him***. (Romans 5:9)

Be of the same mind one toward another. <u>Mind not high things</u>, but <u>condescend to men of low estate</u>. <u>Be not wise in your own conceits</u>. <u>Recompense to no man evil for evil</u>. <u>Provide things honest</u> in the sight of all men. If it be possible, as much as lieth in you, <u>live peaceably with all men</u>. Dearly beloved, *avenge not yourselves,* but rather give place unto **WRATH**: for it is written, ***Vengeance is mine; I will repay, saith the Lord.*** Therefore if thine enemy hunger, <u>*feed him*</u>; if he thirst, <u>*give him drink*</u>: for in so doing thou shalt heap coals of fire on his head. <u>Be not overcome of evil</u>, *but **overcome evil with good***. (Romans 12:16-21)

For I fear, lest, when I come, I shall not find you such as I would, and that I shall be found unto you such as ye would not: lest there be <u>debates</u>, <u>envyings</u>, **WRATHS,** <u>strifes</u>, <u>backbitings</u>, <u>whisperings</u>, <u>swellings</u>, <u>tumults</u>: And lest, when I come again, my God will humble me among you, and that I shall bewail many which have <u>sinned</u> already, and have **not repented** of the <u>uncleanness</u>

and fornication and lasciviousness which they have committed. (2 Corinthians 12:20-21)

Now the **works of the flesh** are manifest, which are these; Adultery, fornication, uncleanness, lasciviousness, Idolatry, witchcraft, hatred, variance, emulations, **WRATH**, strife, seditions, heresies, Envyings, murders, drunkenness, revellings, and such like: of the which I tell you before, as I have also told you in time past, that **they which *do* such things shall *not* inherit the kingdom of God.** (Galatians 5:19)

Wherein in time past ye walked according to the course of this *world*, according to the prince of the power of the air, the spirit that now worketh in the **children of disobedience**: Among whom also we all had our conversation in times past in the lusts of our flesh, fulfilling the desires of the flesh and of the mind; and **were by nature the children of WRATH**, even as others. (Ephesians 2:2-3)

If so be that ye have heard him, and have been taught by him, as the truth is in Jesus: That ye **put off** concerning the former conversation **the old man**, which is corrupt according to the deceitful lusts; And *be renewed in the spirit of your mind*; And that ye ***put on* the new man**, which after God is created in *righteousness* and *true holiness*. Wherefore **putting away** lying, speak every man *truth* with his neighbour: for we are members one of another. Be ye angry, and sin not: let not the sun go down upon your **WRATH**: Neither give place to the devil. Let him that stole *steal no more*: but rather let him labour, working with his hands the thing which is good, *that he may have to give to him that needeth*. Let no corrupt communication proceed out of your mouth, but that which is good to the use of *edifying*, that it may minister grace unto the hearers. And grieve not the holy Spirit of God, whereby ye are sealed unto the day of redemption. Let all bitterness, and **WRATH**, and anger, and clamour, and evil speaking, be put away from you, with all malice: And *be ye kind* one to another, *tenderhearted, forgiving one another*, even as God for Christ's sake hath forgiven you. (Ephesians 4:21-32)

Be ye therefore followers of God, as dear children; And *walk in love*, as Christ also hath loved us, and hath given himself for us an offering and a sacrifice to God for a sweetsmelling savour. ***But*** fornication, and all uncleanness, or covetousness, let it not be once named among you, as becometh saints; ***Neither*** filthiness, nor foolish talking, nor jesting, which are not convenient: but *rather giving of thanks*. For this ye know, that ***no*** whoremonger, ***nor*** unclean person, ***nor*** covetous man, who is an idolater, **hath any inheritance in the kingdom of Christ and of God.** ***Let no man deceive you*** with vain words: for because of these things cometh the **WRATH of God upon the children of disobedience**. (Romans 5:1-6)

Mortify therefore your members which are upon the earth; fornication, uncleanness, inordinate affection, evil concupiscence, and covetousness, which is idolatry: For which things' sake **the WRATH of**

God cometh on the children of disobedience: In the which ye also walked some time, when ye lived in them. But now ye also **put off** all these; anger, **WRATH**, malice, blasphemy, filthy communication out of your mouth. Lie not one to another, seeing that ye have **put off** the old man with his deeds; (Colossians 3:3-9)

And to wait for his Son from heaven, whom he raised from the dead, even *Jesus, which delivered us from the* **WRATH** *to come.* (1 Thessalonians 1:10)

Who both killed the Lord Jesus, *and* their own prophets, *and* have persecuted us; *and* they please not God, *and* are contrary to all men: Forbidding us to speak to the Gentiles *that they might be saved,* to fill up their sins alway: **for the WRATH is come upon them to the uttermost.** (1 Thessalonians 2:15-16)

When your fathers tempted me, proved me, and saw my works forty years. *Wherefore I was grieved with that generation,* and said, **They do** *alway* **err in their** *heart***; and they have not known my ways.** So I sware in my **WRATH**, They shall not enter into my rest.) Take heed, brethren, lest there be in any of you an evil heart of unbelief, in departing from the living God. But exhort one another daily, while it is called To day; **lest any of you be** *hardened* **through the** *deceitfulness* **of sin.** (Hebrews 3:9-13)

Let us therefore *fear, lest,* a promise being left us of entering into his rest, any of you should seem to **come short** of it. For unto us was the gospel preached, as well as unto them: but **the word preached did *not* profit them,** not being mixed with faith in them that heard it. For *we which have believed do enter into rest*, as he said, As I have sworn in my **WRATH**, if they shall enter into my rest: although the works were finished from the foundation of the world. (Hebrews 4:1-3)

Wherefore, my beloved brethren, let every man be *swift to hear, slow to speak, slow to* **WRATH: For the WRATH of man worketh *not* the righteousness of God.** Wherefore **lay apart all** filthiness and superfluity of naughtiness, and *receive* with meekness the engrafted word, which is able to save your souls. But be ye *doers* of the word, and not hearers only, *deceiving* **your own selves.** (James 1:19-22)

And I beheld when he had opened the *sixth seal*, and, lo, there was a great earthquake; and the sun became black as sackcloth of hair, and the moon became as blood; And the stars of heaven fell unto the earth, even as a fig tree casteth her untimely figs, when she is shaken of a mighty wind. And the heaven departed as a scroll when it is rolled together; and every mountain and island were moved out of their places. And **the kings** of the earth, and **the great men**, and **the rich men**, and **the chief captains**, and **the mighty men**, and **every bondman**, and **every free man**, *hid themselves* in the dens and in the rocks of the mountains; And said to the mountains and rocks, Fall on us, and hide us from the face of him that sitteth on the throne, and from the **WRATH *of the Lamb:*** For the great day

of his WRATH is come; and who shall be able to stand? (Revelation 6:12-17)

And the *seventh angel* sounded; and there were great voices in heaven, saying, *The kingdoms of this world are become the kingdoms of our Lord, and of his Christ; and he shall reign for ever and ever.* And *the four and twenty elders*, which sat before God on their seats, fell upon their faces, and worshipped God, Saying, *We give thee thanks, O LORD God Almighty, which art, and wast, and art to come; because thou hast taken to thee thy great power, and hast reigned.* **And the nations were angry, and thy WRATH is come, and the time of the dead, that they should be judged,** and that thou shouldest give *reward* unto thy servants *the prophets*, and to *the saints*, and *them that fear thy name*, small and great; and shouldest **destroy them which destroy the earth.** And the temple of God was opened in heaven, and there was seen in his *temple the ark of his testament*: and there were lightnings, and voices, and thunderings, and an earthquake, and great hail. Revelation (11:15-19)

And **the great dragon** was cast out, that old **serpent**, called the **Devil**, and **Satan, which deceiveth the whole world:** he was cast out into the earth, and his angels were cast out with him. And I heard a loud voice saying in heaven, Now is come salvation, and strength, and the kingdom of our God, and the power of his Christ: *for* **the** *accuser* **of our brethren is cast down**, which accused them before our God day and night. And *they overcame him* by the blood of the Lamb, *and* by the word of their testimony; and *they loved not their lives unto the death.* Therefore rejoice, ye heavens, and ye that dwell in them. *Woe* to the inhabiters of the earth and of the sea! for the devil is come down unto you, having great **WRATH**, because he knoweth that he hath but a short time. And when the dragon saw that he was cast unto the earth, he persecuted the woman which brought forth the man child. *And to the woman were given two wings of a great eagle, that she might fly into the wilderness, into her place, where she is nourished for a time, and times, and half a time, from the face of the serpent.* And the serpent cast out of his mouth water as a flood after the woman, that he might cause her to be carried away of the flood. And *the earth helped the woman,* and the earth opened her mouth, and swallowed up the flood which the dragon cast out of his mouth. And the dragon was **WROTH** with the woman, and went to make war with the remnant of **her seed,** which keep the commandments of God, and have the testimony of Jesus Christ. (Revelation 12:9-17)

And there followed another angel, saying, **Babylon is fallen, is fallen, that great city, because she made all nations drink of the wine of the WRATH of her** *fornication.* And the *third angel* followed them, saying with a loud voice, **If any man** *worship* **the beast and his image, and** *receive his mark* **in his forehead, or in his hand, The same shall drink of the wine of the WRATH of God, which is poured out without mixture into the cup of his indignation; and he shall be tormented with fire and brimstone in the presence of the holy angels, and in**

the presence of the Lamb: And the smoke of their torment ascendeth up for ever and ever: and they have **no rest day nor night**, who *worship* **the beast and his image, and whosoever receiveth** *the mark* **of his name.** (Revelation 14:8-11)

And I looked, and behold a <u>white cloud</u>, and upon the cloud one sat like unto the **Son of man**, having on his head a golden crown, and in his hand a sharp sickle. And <u>another angel</u> came out of the temple, crying with a loud voice to him that sat on the cloud, **Thrust in thy sickle, and** *reap*: **for the time is come for thee to reap; for the harvest of the earth is ripe.** And he that sat on the cloud thrust in his sickle on the earth; and the earth was reaped. And <u>another angel</u> came out of *the temple* which is in heaven, he also having a sharp sickle. And <u>another angel</u> came out from *the altar*, which had power over fire; and cried with a loud cry to him that had the sharp sickle, saying, *Thrust in thy sharp sickle, and gather the clusters of the vine of the earth; for her grapes are fully ripe.* And the angel thrust in his sickle into the earth, and gathered the vine of the earth, and **cast it into the great winepress of the WRATH of God.** And the winepress was trodden without the city, and blood came out of the winepress, even unto the horse bridles, by the space of a thousand and six hundred furlongs. (Revelation 14:14-20)

And I saw another sign in heaven, great and marvellous, <u>seven angels</u> having the **seven last plagues; for in them is filled up the WRATH of God.** (Revelation 15:1)

And after that I looked, and, behold, the temple of the tabernacle of the testimony in heaven was opened: And the *seven angels* came out of the temple, having the *seven plagues,* clothed in pure and white linen, and having their breasts girded with golden girdles. And one of the four beasts gave unto the seven angels **seven golden vials full of the WRATH of God,** who liveth for ever and ever. And the temple was filled with smoke from the glory of God, and from his power; and no man was able to enter into the temple, till the seven plagues of the seven angels were fulfilled. (Revelation 15:5-8)

And I heard a great voice out of the temple saying to the *seven angels*, Go your ways, and **pour out the vials of the WRATH of God upon the earth.** And the first went, and poured out his vial upon the earth; and there fell a noisome and grievous *sore* upon the men which **had the mark of the beast**, and upon them which **worshipped his image**. And the *second angel* poured out his vial upon the *sea*; and it became as the *blood* of a dead man: and every living soul died in the sea. And the *third angel* poured out his vial upon the rivers and fountains of waters; and they became *blood*. And I heard the angel of the waters say, ***Thou art righteous, O Lord, which art, and wast, and shalt be, because thou hast judged thus.* For they have shed the blood of saints and prophets, and thou hast given them blood to drink; for they are worthy.** And I heard another out of the altar say, Even so, Lord God Almighty, true and righteous are thy judgments. And the *fourth angel* poured out his vial upon the sun; and power was given unto him to *scorch men* with fire. And men were scorched with great heat, and blasphemed the name of God, which hath power over these plagues: and they repented not to give him glory. And the *fifth angel* poured out his vial upon **the seat of the beast**; and *his kingdom was full of darkness*; and they gnawed their tongues for pain, And blasphemed the God of heaven because of their *pains and their sores*, and **repented not** of their deeds. And the *sixth angel* poured out his vial upon the great river Euphrates; and *the water thereof was dried up*, that the way of the kings of the east might be prepared. And I saw three unclean spirits like *frogs* come out of the mouth of **the dragon**, and out of the mouth of **the beast**, and out of the mouth of **the false prophet. For they are the spirits of devils, working miracles,** which go forth unto the kings of the earth and of the whole world, to gather them to the battle of that great day of God Almighty. *Behold, I come as a thief.* **Blessed** is he that watcheth, and keepeth his garments, lest he walk naked, and they see his shame. And he gathered them together into a place called in the Hebrew tongue **Armageddon.** And the *seventh angel* poured out his vial into the air; and there came a *great voice out of the temple of heaven,* from the throne, saying, *It is done.* And there were voices, and thunders, and lightnings; and there was a great earthquake, *such as was not since men were upon the earth, so mighty an earthquake, and so great.* **And *the great city* was divided into three parts, and the cities of the nations fell:** and great Babylon came in remembrance before God, to give unto her the cup of the wine of the fierceness of his

WRATH. And every island fled away, and the mountains were not found. And there fell upon men a great hail out of heaven, every stone about the weight of a talent: and men **blasphemed God** because of the plague of the hail; for the plague thereof was exceeding great. (Revelation 16:1-21)

And after these things I saw *another angel* come down from heaven, having great power; and the earth was lightened with his glory. And he cried mightily with a strong voice, saying, **Babylon** the **great is fallen, is fallen,** and is become the habitation of devils, and the hold of every foul spirit, and a cage of every unclean and hateful bird. **For** *all* **nations have drunk of the wine of the WRATH of her fornication, and the kings of the earth have committed fornication with her,** and the **merchants** of the earth are waxed rich through the abundance of her delicacies. And I heard another voice from heaven, saying, *Come out of her, my people, that ye be not partakers of her sins, and that ye receive not of her plagues.* For her sins have reached unto heaven, and *God hath remembered her iniquities.* Reward her even as she rewarded you, and double unto her double according to her works: in the cup which she hath filled fill to her double. How much she hath glorified herself, and lived deliciously, so much torment and sorrow give her: for she saith in her heart, **I sit a queen,** *and* **am no widow,** and shall see no sorrow. Therefore shall her plagues come in one day, death, and mourning, and famine; and **she shall be utterly burned with** *fire*: for strong is the Lord God who judgeth her. And **the kings** of the earth, who have committed <u>fornication</u> and <u>lived deliciously</u> with her, shall bewail her, and lament for her, when they shall see the smoke of her burning, Standing afar off for the fear of her torment, saying, Alas, **alas that great city Babylon,** that mighty city! for in one hour is thy judgment come. (Revelation 18:1-10)

And I saw heaven opened, and behold a white horse; and he that sat upon him was called ***Faithful and True,*** and *in righteousness he doth **judge** and **make war.*** His <u>*eyes*</u> were as a flame of fire, and on his head were *<u>many crowns</u>*; and he had a *name* written, that no man knew, but he himself. And he was clothed with <u>*a vesture dipped in blood*</u>: and *his name is called* ***The Word of God****.* And ***the armies*** which were in heaven followed him upon white horses, clothed in fine linen, white and clean. And out of his mouth goeth a <u>*sharp sword*</u>, that with it he should **smite the nations**: and **he shall rule them with a <u>rod of iron</u>: and he treadeth the winepress of the fierceness and WRATH of Almighty God.** And he hath on his vesture and on his thigh a name written, **KING OF KINGS, AND LORD OF LORDS**. (Revelation 9:11-16)

Chapter 23

BURN

And now also the axe is laid unto the root of the trees: **therefore every tree which bringeth not forth good fruit is hewn down, and cast into the fire.** I indeed baptize you with water unto repentance. but he that cometh after me is mightier than I, whose shoes I am not worthy to bear: he shall baptize you with the Holy Ghost, and with fire: Whose fan is in his hand, and *he will throughly purge his floor*, and gather his **wheat** into the <u>garner</u>; *but* **he will BURN up the <u>chaff</u> with unquenchable fire.** (Matthew 3:10-12)

Another parable put he forth unto them, saying, The kingdom of heaven is likened unto *a man which sowed **good seed** in his field:* But while men slept, <u>his enemy came and sowed</u> **tares** among the wheat, and went his way. But when the blade was sprung up, and brought forth fruit, then appeared the tares also. So the servants of the householder came and said unto him, Sir, didst not thou sow good seed in thy field? from whence then hath it tares? He said unto them, **An enemy hath done this.** The servants said unto him, Wilt thou then that we go and gather them up? But he said, Nay; lest while ye gather up the tares, ye root up also the wheat with them. <u>Let both grow together until the harvest: and in the time of harvest I will say to the reapers</u>, **Gather ye together first the <u>tares</u>, and bind them in bundles to BURN them:** *but gather the <u>wheat</u> into my barn.* (Matthew 13:24-30)

Then Jesus sent the multitude away, and went into the house: and his disciples came unto him, saying, *Declare unto us the parable of the tares of the field.* He answered and said unto them, He that soweth the good seed is the Son of man; **The field is the world;** the <u>good seed</u> are the children of the kingdom; but the **<u>tares</u> are the children of the wicked one; The <u>enemy</u> that sowed them is the devil;** the <u>harvest is the end of the world</u>; and the <u>reapers are the angels</u>. **As therefore the <u>tares</u> are gathered and <u>BURNED</u> in the fire; so shall it be in the end of this world.** The Son of man shall send forth his angels, and they shall gather out of his kingdom *all* **things that** <u>offend</u>**,** *and* **them which <u>do iniquity</u>; And shall cast them into a furnace of fire: there shall be wailing and gnashing of teeth.** (Matthew 13:36-42)

And Jesus answered and spake unto them again by parables, and said, The kingdom of heaven is like unto *a certain king, which made a marriage for his son,* And sent forth his servants to call them that were bidden to the wedding: and <u>they would not come</u>. Again, he sent forth other servants, saying, Tell them which are bidden, Behold, I have prepared my dinner: my oxen and my fatlings are killed, and all things are ready: come unto the marriage. But <u>they made light of it</u>, and went their ways, one to his farm, another to his merchandise: And <u>the remnant took his servants, and entreated them spitefully, and slew them</u>. But when the king heard thereof, *he was wroth:* and he sent forth his armies, and **destroyed those <u>murderers</u>, and BURNED up their city.** Then saith he to his servants, *The wedding is ready, but* **they which were bidden were not worthy.** (Matthew 22:1-8)

And as the people were in expectation, and all men mused in their hearts of John, whether he were the Christ, or not; John answered, saying unto them all, I indeed baptize you with water; but one mightier than I cometh, the latchet of whose shoes I am not worthy to unloose: he shall baptize you with the Holy Ghost and with fire: Whose fan is in his hand, and *he will throughly purge his floor,* and ***will gather the wheat into his garner;* but the chaff he will BURN with fire unquenchable.** (Luke 3:15-17)

I am the true vine, and my Father is the husbandman. **Every branch in me that beareth not fruit he taketh away:** *and every branch that beareth fruit, he purgeth it, that it may bring forth more fruit.* Now ye are clean through the word which I have spoken unto you. *Abide in me, and I in you.* As the branch cannot bear fruit of itself, except it abide in the vine; no more can ye, except ye *abide in me.* I am the vine, ye are the branches: He that *abideth in me,* and I in him, the same bringeth forth *much fruit:* **for without me ye can do nothing. If a man abide *not* in me, he is cast forth as a branch, and is withered; and men gather them, and cast them into the fire, and they are BURNED.** (John 15:1-6)

And many that believed came, and confessed, and shewed their deeds. Many of them also which used **curious arts** (occult/black magic) brought their **books** together, and **BURNED** them before all men:

and they counted the price of them, and found it fifty thousand pieces of silver. (Acts 19:18-19)

For this cause **God gave them up unto vile affections:** for even their women did change the natural use into that which is against nature: And likewise also the men, leaving the natural use of the woman, **BURNED** in their lust one toward another; men with men working that which is unseemly, and receiving in themselves that recompence of their error which was meet. And even as they did *not* like to retain God in their knowledge, **God gave them over to a reprobate mind,** to do those things which are not convenient; Being filled with *all* unrighteousness, fornication, wickedness, covetousness, maliciousness; full of envy, murder, debate, deceit, malignity; whisperers, Backbiters, haters of God, despiteful, proud, boasters, inventors of evil things, disobedient to parents, Without understanding, covenantbreakers, without natural affection, implacable, unmerciful: **Who knowing the judgment of God, that they which commit such things are worthy of death,** not only do the same, *but* have *pleasure* in them that do them. (Acts 1:26-32)

If any man's work shall be **BURNED**, he shall suffer loss: but he himself shall be saved; yet so as by fire. (1 Corinthians 3:15)

And though I bestow all my goods to feed the poor, and though I give my body to be **BURNED**, and **have *not* charity, it profiteth me nothing.** (1 Corinthians 13:3)

For **it is impossible** for those who were once enlightened, and have tasted of the heavenly gift, and were made partakers of the Holy Ghost, And have tasted the good word of God, and the powers of the world to come, *If they shall fall away,* **to renew them again unto repentance; seeing** they crucify to themselves the Son of God afresh, **and** *put him to an open shame.* For the earth which drinketh in the rain that cometh oft upon it, and bringeth forth herbs meet for them by whom it is dressed, receiveth blessing from God: *But* **that which beareth thorns and briers is** rejected, **and is nigh unto cursing; whose end is to be BURNED.** (Hebrews 6:4-8)

But **the rich,** in that he is made low: because as the flower of the grass he shall pass away. For the sun is no sooner risen with a **BURNING** heat, but it withereth the grass, and the flower thereof falleth, and the grace of the fashion of it perisheth: **so also shall the rich man fade away in his ways.** (James 1:10-11)

The Lord is not slack concerning his promise, as some men count slackness; but *is longsuffering to us-ward, not willing that* **any** *should perish, but that all should come to repentance.* But the day of *the Lord will come as a thief in the night;* in the which the heavens shall pass away with a great noise, and the elements shall melt with fervent heat, **the earth also and the works that are therein shall be BURNED up.** (2 Peter 3:9-10)

And in the midst of the _seven candlesticks_ one like unto the *Son of man,* clothed with a garment down to the foot, and girt about the paps with a golden girdle. His head and his hairs were white like wool, as white as snow; and his eyes were as a flame of fire; And his feet like unto fine brass, as if they **BURNED** in a furnace; and his voice as the sound of many waters. And he had in his right hand _seven stars_: and out of his _mouth_ went a _sharp twoedged sword_: and _his countenance_ was as the sun shineth in his strength. <u>And when I saw him, I fell at his feet as dead</u>. And he laid his right hand upon me, saying unto me, **Fear not; I am the first and the last: I am he that liveth, and was dead; and, behold, I am alive for evermore, Amen; and have the keys of hell and of death.** (Revelation 1:13-18)

And the _seven angels_ which had the _seven trumpets_ prepared themselves to sound. The <u>_first angel_</u> sounded, and there followed <u>hail and fire</u> mingled with <u>blood</u>, and they were cast upon the earth: and the <u>third part of _trees_</u> was **BURNT** up, and <u>all green grass</u> was **BURNT** up. And the <u>_second angel_</u> sounded, and as it were a <u>great mountain **BURNING** with fire</u> was cast into the sea: and the <u>third part of the _sea_ became blood</u>; And the <u>third part of the _creatures_</u> which were in the sea, and had life, <u>died</u>; and the <u>third part of the _ships_ were destroyed</u>. And the <u>_third angel_</u> sounded, and there <u>fell a great star from heaven</u>, **BURNING** as it were a lamp, and it <u>fell upon the third part of the _rivers_</u>, and upon the <u>fountains of _waters_</u>; **And the name of the star is called <u>Wormwood</u>:** and the <u>third part of the waters became **wormwood**</u>; and many men died of the *waters*, because they were made bitter. And the *fourth angel* sounded, and the third part of the *sun* was smitten, and the third part of the *moon*, and the third part of the *stars*; so as the third part of them was *darkened*, and the day shone not for a third part of it, and the night likewise. And I beheld, and heard an angel flying through the midst of heaven, saying with a loud voice, **Woe, woe, woe, to the inhabiters of the earth by reason of the other voices of the trumpet of the three angels, which are *yet* to sound!** (Revelation 8:6-13)

Chapter 24

FLAME

There was a certain rich man, which was <u>clothed in purple and fine linen</u>, and <u>fared sumptuously every day</u>: And *there was a certain beggar named Lazarus,* which was laid at his gate, <u>full of sores,</u> And <u>desiring to be fed with the crumbs</u> which fell from the rich man's table: moreover <u>the dogs came and licked his sores</u>. And it came to pass, that the *beggar died, and was carried by the angels into Abraham's bosom:* <u>the rich man also died, and was buried</u>; **And in hell he lift up his eyes, being in torments,** and seeth Abraham afar off, and Lazarus in his bosom. And he cried and said, Father Abraham, have mercy on me, and send Lazarus, that he may dip the tip of his finger in water, and cool my tongue; for **I am tormented in this FLAME**. But Abraham said, **Son, remember that thou in thy lifetime receivedst thy good things, and likewise Lazarus evil things: but now he is comforted, and thou art tormented.** And beside all this, <u>between us and you there is a great gulf fixed</u>: so that they which would pass from hence to you cannot; neither can they pass to us, that would come from thence. Then he said, I pray thee therefore, father, that thou wouldest send him to my father's house: For I have five brethren; that he may testify unto them, lest they also come into this place of torment. Abraham saith unto him, *They have*

*Moses and the prophets; **let them hear them.*** And he said, Nay, father Abraham: but if one went unto them from the dead, they will **repent**. And he said unto him, ***If* they hear *not* Moses and the prophets, neither will they be persuaded, though one rose from the dead.** (Luke 16:19-31)

And in the midst of the <u>seven candlesticks</u> one like unto *the Son of man*, clothed with a garment down to the foot, and girt about the paps with a golden girdle. His head and his hairs were white like wool, as white as snow; and his eyes were as a **FLAME** of fire; And his feet like unto fine brass, as if they burned in a furnace; and his voice as the sound of many waters. And he had *<u>in his right hand seven stars</u>*: and out of his mouth went a *<u>sharp twoedged sword</u>*: and his countenance was as the sun shineth in his strength. And when I saw him, <u>I fell at his feet as dead</u>. And he laid his right hand upon me, saying unto me, *Fear not; I am the first and the last: I am he that liveth, and was dead; and, behold, I am alive for evermore, Amen; and have the keys of hell and of death.* (Revelation 1:13-18)

And unto the angel of the <u>church in Thyatira</u> write; These things saith the Son of God, who hath his eyes like unto a **FLAME** of fire, and his feet are like fine brass; *I know thy works*, and <u>charity</u>, and <u>service</u>, and <u>faith</u>, and thy <u>patience</u>, and thy <u>works</u>; and the last to be more than the first. *Notwithstanding I have a few things against thee,* **because thou sufferest that woman Jezebel, which** *calleth* **herself a prophetess, to teach and to seduce my servants to commit** *fornication***, and to eat things**

sacrificed unto idols. And *I gave her space to repent of her fornication;* and **she repented** *not.* Behold, I will cast her into a bed, and them that commit adultery with her into great tribulation, except they repent of their deeds. And I will kill her children with death; and all the churches shall know that *I am he which searcheth the reins and hearts: and I will give unto every one of you according to your works.* (Revelation 2:18-23)

And I saw heaven opened, and behold a <u>white horse</u>; and he that sat upon him was called *Faithful and True*, and in righteousness *he doth judge and make war.* His *eyes* were as a **FLAME** of fire, and on his *head* were <u>many crowns</u>; and he had a *name* written, that no man knew, but he himself. And he was clothed with <u>a vesture dipped in blood</u>: and his name is called **The Word of God**. And the *armies* which were in heaven followed him upon white horses, clothed in fine linen, white and clean. And out of his *mouth* goeth a <u>sharp sword</u>, that with it he should <u>smite the nations</u>: and *he shall rule them with a <u>rod of iron</u>: and he treadeth the winepress of the fierceness and <u>wrath of Almighty God</u>.* And he hath on his vesture and on his thigh a name written, KING OF KINGS, AND LORD OF LORDS. (Revelation 19:11-16)

Chapter 25

BLACK

But these speak evil of those things which they know not: but what they know naturally, as brute beasts, in those things **they corrupt themselves. Woe** unto them! for they have gone in the way of Cain, and ran greedily after the error of Balaam for reward, and perished in the gainsaying of Core. These are spots in your feasts of charity, when they feast with you, feeding themselves without fear: clouds they are without water, carried about of winds; trees whose fruit withereth, without fruit, twice dead, plucked up by the roots; Raging waves of the sea, foaming out their own shame; wandering stars, **to whom is reserved the BLACKNESS of darkness for ever.** (Jude 1:10-13)

But these, **as natural brute beasts, made to be taken and destroyed,** speak evil of the things that they understand not; and shall utterly perish in their own corruption; And **shall receive the reward of unrighteousness,** as they that count it pleasure to riot in the day time. Spots they are and blemishes, **sporting themselves with** *their own deceivings* while they feast with you; Having eyes full of adultery, and that **cannot cease from sin**; beguiling unstable souls: an heart they have exercised with covetous practices; **cursed children:** Which have forsaken the right way, and are gone astray, following the way of Balaam the son of Bosor, who

loved the wages of *un*righteousness; But was rebuked for his iniquity: the dumb ass speaking with man's voice forbad the madness of the prophet. These are wells without water, clouds that are carried with a tempest; **to whom the mist of darkness (BLACKEST darkness/NIV) is reserved for ever.** For when they speak great swelling words of vanity, they *allure* through the lusts of the flesh, through much wantonness, those that were clean escaped from them who live in error. *While* they promise them liberty, **they themselves are the servants of corruption:** for of whom a man is **overcome**, of the same is he brought in **bondage**. For *if after* they have escaped the pollutions of the world through the knowledge of the Lord and Saviour Jesus Christ, **they are *again* entangled therein, and overcome, the latter end is worse with them than the beginning.** For it had been *better* for them *not* to have known the way of righteousness, than, after they have known it, to **turn from the holy commandment delivered unto them**. But it is happened unto them according to the *true proverb*, **The dog is turned to his own vomit again; and the sow that was washed to her wallowing in the mire.** (2 Peter 2:12-22)

CHAPTER 26

SCORCH

And he spake many things unto them in parables, saying, *Behold, a sower went forth to sow;* And when he sowed, some seeds fell by the way side, and the *fowls* came and devoured them up: Some fell upon **stony places,** where they had not much earth: and forthwith they sprung up, because they had no deepness of earth: And when the sun was up, they were **SCORCHED**; and *because* they had no root, they withered away. And some fell among **thorns;** and the thorns sprung up, and choked them: But other fell into **good ground**, and brought forth fruit, some an *hundredfold,* some *sixtyfold,* some *thirtyfold.* **Who hath ears to hear, let him hear.** (Matthew 13:3-9)

And he taught them many things by parables, and said unto them in his doctrine, Hearken; Behold, *there went out a sower to sow:* And it came to pass, as he sowed, some fell by **the way side**, and the *fowls* of the air came and devoured it up. And some fell on **stony ground,** where it had not much earth; and immediately it sprang up, because it had no depth of earth: But when the sun was up, it was **SCORCHED**; and because it had no root, it withered away. And some fell among **thorns,** and the thorns grew up, and choked it, and it yielded **no fruit.** And other fell on **good ground**, *and did yield* *fruit that sprang up and increased; and brought forth, some <u>thirty</u>, and some <u>sixty</u>, and some an <u>hundred</u>.* And he said unto them, **He that hath ears to hear, let him hear.** (Mark 4:2-9)

And I heard **a great voice out of the temple** saying to the <u>seven angels</u>, **Go your ways, and pour out the *vials of the wrath of God* upon the earth**. And the <u>first</u> went, and poured out his vial upon the <u>earth</u>; and there fell a noisome and *grievous sore* upon the men which had **the mark of the beast**, and upon them which **worshipped his image**. And the <u>second angel</u> poured out his vial upon the <u>sea</u>; and it became as the *blood* of a dead man: and every living soul died in the sea. And the <u>third angel</u> poured out his vial upon the <u>rivers and fountains</u> of waters; and they became *blood*. And I heard the angel of the waters say, *Thou art righteous, O Lord, which art, and wast, and shalt be, because thou hast judged thus.* **For they have shed the blood of saints and prophets, *and thou hast given them blood to drink; for they are worthy.*** And I heard another out of the altar say, **Even so, Lord God Almighty, true and righteous are thy judgments.** And the <u>fourth angel</u> poured out his vial upon the <u>sun</u>; and power was given unto him to **SCORCH** *men with fire*. And men were **SCORCHED** with great heat, and <u>blasphemed the name of God</u>, which hath power over these plagues: and **they repented *not* to give him glory.** (Revelation 16:1-9)

Chapter 27

WORM DIETH NOT

And **whosoever shall <u>offend</u> one of these little ones that believe in me,** it is better for him that a millstone were hanged about his neck, and he were cast into the sea. And <u>if thy **hand** offend thee,</u> *cut it off:* it is better for thee to enter into life maimed, than having two hands to go into **hell, into the fire that never shall be quenched: Where their WORM DIETH NOT, and the fire is not quenched.** And <u>if thy **foot** offend thee,</u> *cut it off:* it is better for thee to enter halt into life, than having two feet to be cast into **hell, into the fire that never shall be quenched: Where their WORM DIETH NOT, and the fire is not quenched.** And <u>if thine **eye** offend thee,</u> *pluck it out:* it is better for thee to enter into the kingdom of God with one eye, than having two eyes to be cast into **hell fire: Where their WORM DIETH NOT, and the fire is not quenched.** (Mark 9:42-48)

Chapter 28

JUDGEMENT

Ye have heard that it was said of them of old time, Thou shalt not kill; and whosoever shall kill shall be in danger of the **JUDGMENT:** But I say unto you, That whosoever is angry with his brother without a cause shall be in danger of the **JUDGMENT:** and whosoever shall say to his brother, Raca, shall be in danger of the council: but whosoever shall say, Thou fool, **shall be in danger of hell fire**. Therefore if thou bring thy gift to the altar, and there rememberest that thy brother hath ought against thee; Leave there thy gift before the altar, and go thy way; *first be reconciled to thy brother, and then come and offer thy gift.* (Matthew 5:21-24)

For with what JUDGMENT ye judge, ye shall be judged: and with what measure ye mete, it shall be measured to you again. (Matthew 7:2)

And whosoever shall not receive you, nor hear your words, when ye depart out of that house or city, shake off the dust of your feet. Verily I say unto you, **It shall be more tolerable for the land of Sodom and Gomorrha in** *the day of* **JUDGMENT, than for that city.** (Matthew 10:14-15)

Then began he to upbraid the cities wherein most of his mighty works were done, *because* **they repented**

JUDGEMENT / 171

***not*: Woe** unto thee, <u>Chorazin</u>! **woe** unto thee, <u>Bethsaida</u>! for if the mighty works, which were done in you, had been done in Tyre and Sidon, *they would have repented long ago in sackcloth and ashes.* But I say unto you, It shall be more tolerable for Tyre and Sidon at the day of **JUDGMENT**, than for you. And thou, <u>Capernaum</u>, <u>which art exalted unto heaven</u>, **shalt be brought down to hell:** for if the mighty works, which have been done in thee, had been done in Sodom, it would have remained until this day. But I say unto you, **That it shall be more tolerable for the land of Sodom in the day of JUDGMENT, than for thee.** (Matthew 11:20-24)

That it might be fulfilled which was spoken by Esaias the prophet, saying, <u>*Behold my servant*</u>, *whom I have chosen; my beloved, in whom my soul is well pleased:* I will put my spirit upon him, and **he shall shew JUDGMENT to the Gentiles**. He shall not strive, nor cry; neither shall any man hear his voice in the streets. A bruised reed shall he not break, and smoking flax shall he not quench, till **he send forth JUDGMENT unto victory**. And in his name shall the Gentiles trust. (Matthew 12:17-21)

<u>O generation of vipers</u>, how can ye, being evil, speak good things? *for out of the abundance of the heart the mouth speaketh.* A <u>good man</u> out of the good treasure of the heart bringeth forth ***good things:*** and an <u>evil man</u> out of the evil treasure bringeth forth **evil things**. But I say unto you, That **every idle word** that men shall speak, they shall give account thereof in the day of **JUDGMENT**. *For by*

thy words thou shalt be justified, and **by thy words thou shalt be condemned.** (Matthew 12:34-36)

Then certain of the scribes and of the Pharisees answered, saying, *Master, we would see a sign from thee.* But he answered and said unto them, An evil and adulterous generation seeketh after a sign; and there shall no sign be given to it, but the sign of the prophet Jonas: For as Jonas was three days and three nights in the whale's belly; so shall the Son of man be three days and three nights in the heart of the earth. The men of Nineveh shall rise in **JUDGMENT** with this generation, and shall **condemn it:** because **they repented at the preaching of Jonas**; and, *behold, a greater than Jonas is here.* The queen of the south shall rise up in the **JUDGMENT** with this generation, and shall **condemn it:** for she came from the uttermost parts of the earth **to hear the wisdom of Solomon;** and, *behold, a greater than Solomon is here.* (Matthew 12:38-42)

Woe unto you, scribes and Pharisees, *hypocrites!* for ye pay tithe of mint and anise and cummin, and **have omitted the weightier matters of the law, JUDGMENT,** *mercy,* and *faith*: these ought ye to have done, and *not* to leave the other undone. Ye blind guides, which strain at a gnat, and swallow a camel. Woe unto you, scribes and Pharisees, *hypocrites!* for ye make clean the outside of the cup and of the platter, but **within they are full of extortion and excess.** Thou blind Pharisee, cleanse first that which is within the cup and platter, that the outside of them may be clean also. Woe unto you, scribes and Pharisees, *hypocrites!* for ye are like unto whited sepulchres, which indeed appear <u>beautiful outward</u>, *but* **are within full of dead men's bones, and of all uncleanness.** Even so ye also <u>outwardly appear righteous unto men</u>, but within ye are **full of hypocrisy and iniquity**. Woe unto you, scribes and Pharisees, *hypocrites!* because ye build the tombs of the prophets, and garnish the sepulchres of the righteous, (Matthew 23:23-29)

And he said unto them, In what place soever ye enter into an house, there abide till ye depart from that place. And <u>whosoever shall not receive you, nor hear you</u>, when ye depart thence, shake off the dust under your feet for a testimony against them. Verily I say unto you, <u>It shall be more tolerable for Sodom and Gomorrha in the day of **JUDGMENT**, than for that city</u>. **And they went out, and preached that men should repent.** (Mark 6:10-12)

But into whatsoever city ye enter, and they receive you not, go your ways out into the streets of the same, and say, Even the very dust of your city, which cleaveth on us, we do wipe off against you: notwithstanding be ye sure of this, that the kingdom of God is come nigh unto you. But I say unto you, that it shall be more tolerable in that day for Sodom, than for that city. **Woe** unto thee, <u>Chorazin</u>! **woe** unto thee, <u>Bethsaida</u>! for if the mighty works had been done in Tyre and Sidon, which have been done in you, *they had a great while ago repented, sitting in sackcloth and ashes.* But it shall be more tolerable for Tyre and Sidon at the **JUDGMENT**, than for you. And thou, <u>Capernaum</u>, which art exalted to heaven, shalt be thrust down to hell. *He that heareth you heareth me;* **and he that despiseth you despiseth me; and he that despiseth me despiseth him that sent me.** (Luke 10:10-16)

And when the people were gathered thick together, he began to say, <u>This is an evil generation: they seek a sign; and there shall no sign be given it, but the sign of Jonas the prophet.</u> For as Jonas was a sign unto the Ninevites, so shall also the Son of man be to this generation. <u>The queen of the south</u> shall rise up in the **JUDGMENT** with the men of this generation, and **condemn them:** for she came from the utmost parts of the earth to hear the wisdom of Solomon; and, ***behold, a greater than Solomon is here.*** The men of Nineve shall rise up in the **JUDGMENT** with this generation, and **shall condemn it:** *for they repented at the preaching of Jonas; and,* ***behold, a greater than Jonas is here.*** (Luke 11:29-32)

And another came, saying, Lord, behold, here is thy pound, which I have kept laid up in a napkin: For I feared thee, because ***thou art an austere man:*** thou takest up that thou layedst not down, and reapest that thou didst not sow. And he saith unto him, **Out of thine own mouth will I JUDGE thee, thou wicked servant. Thou knewest that I was an** *austere man,* **taking up that I laid not down, and reaping that I did not sow:** Wherefore then gavest not thou my money into the bank, that at my coming I might have required mine own with usury? And he said unto them that stood by, Take from him the pound, and give it to him that hath ten pounds. (And they

JUDGEMENT / 175

said unto him, Lord, he hath ten pounds.) For I say unto you, *That unto every one which hath shall be given;* **and from him that hath not, even that he hath shall be taken away from him.** But those mine enemies, which would not that I should reign over them, bring hither, and ***slay them before me.*** (Luke 19:20-27)

For the Father JUDGETH no man, but hath committed all JUDGMENT unto the Son: That all men should honour the Son, even as they honour the Father. **He that honoureth not the Son honoureth not the Father which hath sent him.** Verily, verily, I say unto you, *He that heareth my word, and believeth on him that sent me, hath everlasting life, and shall not come into condemnation; but is passed from death unto life.* Verily, verily, I say unto you, The hour is coming, and now is, when the dead shall hear the voice of the Son of God: and they that hear shall live. *For as the Father hath life in himself; so hath he given to the Son to have life in himself;* And hath **given him authority to execute JUDGMENT** also, because <u>*he is the Son of man*</u>. Marvel not at this: for the hour is coming, in the which all that are in the graves shall hear his voice, And shall come forth; *they that have <u>done good</u>, unto* **the resurrection of life;** *and* they that have <u>done evil</u>, unto the **resurrection of damnation.** *I can of mine own self do nothing: as I hear, I* **JUDGE**: *and my* **JUDGMENT** *is just; because I seek not mine own will, but the will of the Father which hath sent me.* (John 5:22-30)

JUDGEMENT / 176

And yet if I judge, **my judgment is true:** for *I am not alone, but I and the Father that sent me.* (John 8:16)

These words spake Jesus in the treasury, as he taught in the temple: and no man laid hands on him; for his hour was not yet come. Then said Jesus again unto them, I go my way, and ye shall seek me, and shall die in your sins: whither I go, ye cannot come. Then said the Jews, Will he kill himself? because he saith, Whither I go, ye cannot come. And he said unto them, **Ye are from beneath**; *I am from above:* **ye are of this world;** *I am **not** of this world.* **I said therefore unto you, that ye shall die in your sins: for if ye believe *not* that I am he, ye shall die in your sins.** Then said they unto him, Who art thou? And Jesus saith unto them, Even the same that I said unto you from the beginning. I have many things to say and to **JUDGE** of you: but he that sent me is true; and I speak to the world those things which I have heard of him. (John 8:20-26)

Ye are of your father the devil, and the lusts of your father ye will do. He was a murderer from the beginning, and abode not in the truth, because there is *no truth in him*. When he speaketh a *lie*, he speaketh of his own: for he is a *liar*, and the father of it. *And because I tell you the truth, ye believe me not.* Which of you convinceth me of sin? And if I say the truth, why do ye not believe me? *He that is of God heareth God's words:* ye therefore hear them not, *because* **ye are not of God.** Then answered the Jews, and said unto him, Say we not well that thou art a Samaritan, and hast a devil? Jesus answered, I have not a devil; *but I honour my Father*, **and ye do dishonour me.** And *I seek not mine own glory*: there is one that seeketh and **JUDGETH.** (John 8:44-50)

And Jesus said, *For* **JUDGMENT** *I am come into this world,* **that they which see not might see; and that they which see might be made blind.** And some of the Pharisees which were with him heard these words, and said unto him, Are we blind also? Jesus said unto them, If ye were blind, ye should have no sin: but now ye say, We see; therefore your sin remaineth. (John 9:39-41)

Now is the **JUDGMENT** of **this world:** now shall the prince of **this world** be cast out. (John 12:31)

He that rejecteth me, and receiveth not my words, hath one that **JUDGETH** him: **the word that I have spoken, the same shall JUDGE him in the last day.** (John 12:48)

Nevertheless I tell you the truth; It is expedient for you that I go away: for if I go not away, the Comforter will not come unto you; but if I depart, I will send him unto you. And when he is come, **he will reprove the world of sin, and of righteousness, and of JUDGMENT:** Of sin, because they believe not on me; Of righteousness, because I go to my Father, and ye see me no more; Of **JUDGMENT,** because **the prince of this world is JUDGED.** (John 16:7-11)

And *he commanded us to preach unto the people,* and to testify that *it is he which was ordained of God to be the* **JUDGE** *of quick and dead.* (Acts 10:42)

Then Paul and Barnabas waxed bold, and said, It was necessary that the word of God should first have been spoken to you: but seeing ye put it from you, and **JUDGE yourselves unworthy of everlasting life,** lo, we turn to the Gentiles. (Acts 13:46)

And the times of this ignorance God winked at; **but now commandeth all men every where to repent:** Because he hath appointed a day, in the which **he will JUDGE the world in righteousness by that man whom he hath ordained;** whereof he hath given assurance unto all men, in that he hath raised him from the dead. (Acts 17:30-31)

And after certain days, when Felix came with his wife Drusilla, which was a Jewess, he sent for Paul, and heard him concerning the faith in Christ. And as he reasoned of *<u>righteousness</u>*, *<u>temperance</u>*, *and* **JUDGMENT** *to come,* Felix trembled, and answered, Go thy way for this time; when I have a convenient season, I will call for thee. (Acts 24:24-25)

For this cause God gave them up unto vile affections: for even their women did change the natural use into that which is against nature: And likewise also the men, leaving the natural use of the woman, burned in their lust one toward another; men with men working that which is unseemly, and **receiving in themselves that recompence of their error which was meet.** And even as they did not like to retain God in their knowledge, **God gave them over to a reprobate mind,** to do those things which are not convenient; Being *filled* with all unrighteousness, fornication, wickedness, covetousness, maliciousness; full of envy, murder, debate, deceit, malignity; whisperers, Backbiters, haters of God, despiteful, proud, boasters, inventors of evil things, disobedient to parents, Without understanding, covenantbreakers, without natural affection, implacable, unmerciful: Who knowing the **JUDGMENT** of God, **that they which commit such things are worthy of death, not only *do* the same, but have *pleasure* in them that do them.** (Romans 1:26-32)

Therefore thou art inexcusable, O man, whosoever thou art that **JUDGEST**: for wherein thou **JUDGEST** another, thou condemnest thyself; for thou that **JUDGEST** doest the same things. But we are sure that the **JUDGMENT** of God is according to truth against them which commit such things. And thinkest thou this, O man, that **JUDGEST** them which do such things, and doest the same, that thou shalt escape the **JUDGMENT** of God? **Or *despisest* thou the riches of his goodness and forbearance and longsuffering**; not knowing that the

goodness of God leadeth thee to *repentance?* **But after thy hardness and impenitent heart treasurest up unto thyself** *wrath* **against the** *day of wrath* **and revelation of the righteous JUDGMENT of God; Who will render to every man according to his** *deeds:* To them who by patient continuance in <u>well doing</u> seek for glory and honour and immortality, *eternal life:* But unto them that are <u>contentious</u>, and <u>do not obey the truth</u>, but <u>obey **un**righteousness</u>, **indignation** *and* **wrath, Tribulation** *and* **anguish,** upon every soul of man that <u>doeth evil</u>, of the Jew first, and also of the Gentile; But *glory, honour, and peace, to every man that <u>worketh good</u>,* to the Jew first, and also to the Gentile: For there is no respect of persons with God. (Romans 2:1-11)

In the day when **God shall JUDGE the secrets of men** by Jesus Christ according to my gospel. (Romans 2:16)

God forbid: yea, let God be true, but every man a liar; as it is written, That thou mightest be justified in thy sayings, and mightest overcome when thou art **JUDGED**. But if our **un**righteousness commend the righteousness of God, what shall we say? Is God unrighteous **who taketh vengeance?** (I speak as a man) **God forbid:** for then how shall God **JUDGE** the world? For if the truth of God hath more abounded through my lie unto his glory; why yet am I also **JUDGED** as a sinner? And not rather, (as we be slanderously reported, and as some affirm that we say,) Let us do evil, that good may come? **whose damnation is just.** (Romans 3:4-8)

But why dost thou **JUDGE** thy brother? or why dost thou set at nought thy brother? **for we shall all stand before the JUDGMENT seat of Christ.** For it is written, As I live, saith the Lord, <u>every knee shall bow to me, and every tongue shall confess to God.</u> **So then every one of us shall give account of himself to God.** (Romans 14:10-12)

For I know nothing by myself; yet am I not hereby justified: but he that **JUDGETH** me is the Lord. Therefore **JUDGE** nothing before the time, until the Lord come, who both **will bring to light the hidden things of darkness,** *and* **will make manifest the counsels of the hearts:** and then shall every man have praise of God. (1 Corinthians 4:4-5)

I wrote unto you in an epistle **not to company with <u>fornicators</u>:** Yet not altogether with the <u>fornicators of this world</u>, or with the <u>covetous</u>, or <u>extortioners</u>, or with <u>idolaters</u>; for then must ye needs go out of the world. But now I have written unto you not to keep company, **if any man that is called <u>a *brother*</u>** (a Christian) **be a fornicator, or covetous, or an idolator, or a railer, or a drunkard, or an extortioner; <u>with</u> <u>such</u> an <u>one</u> <u>no</u> <u>not</u> <u>to</u> <u>eat</u>.** For what have I to do to **JUDGE** them also that are *without?* ***do not ye* JUDGE** *them that are within?* But them that are without God **JUDGETH. Therefore *put away* from among yourselves that wicked person.** (1 Corinthians 5:9-13)

<u>Dare any of you, having a matter against another, go to law before the unjust, and not before the saints?</u> Do ye not know that *the saints shall*

JUDGEMENT / 182

JUDGE *the world?* and if the world shall be **JUDGED** by you, are ye unworthy to **JUDGE** the smallest matters? *Know ye not that we shall* **JUDGE** *angels? how much more things that pertain to this life?* If then ye have judgments of things pertaining to this life, set them to **JUDGE** who are least esteemed in the church. I speak to your shame. Is it so, that there is not a wise man among you? no, not one that shall be able to **JUDGE** *between his brethren?* But brother goeth to law with brother, *and* that before the unbelievers. Now therefore there is utterly a fault among you, because ye go to law one with another. Why do ye not rather take wrong? why do ye not rather suffer yourselves to be defrauded? Nay, ye do wrong, and defraud, and that your brethren. **Know ye not that the *un*righteous shall *not* inherit the kingdom of God? Be not deceived**: neither fornicators, nor idolaters, nor adulterers, nor effeminate, nor abusers of themselves with mankind, Nor thieves, nor covetous, nor drunkards, nor revilers, nor extortioners, shall inherit the kingdom of God. (1 Corinthians 6:1-10)

For I have received of the Lord that which also I delivered unto you, that the Lord Jesus the same night in which he was betrayed took bread: And when he had given thanks, he brake it, and said, Take, eat: this is my body, which is broken for you: this do in remembrance of me. After the same manner also he took the cup, when he had supped, saying, this cup is the new testament in my blood: this do ye, as oft as ye drink it, in remembrance of me. For as often as ye eat this bread, and drink this cup, ye do shew the Lord's death till he come. **Wherefore whosoever shall eat this bread, and drink this cup of the Lord, *unworthily*, shall be guilty of the body and blood of the Lord.** But let a man *examine himself*, and so let him eat of that bread, and drink of that cup. **For he that eateth and drinketh *unworthily*, eateth and drinketh damnation to himself, not discerning the Lord's body.** For this cause many are weak and sickly among you, and many sleep. For if we would **JUDGE** *ourselves*, we should not be **JUDGED**. But when we are **JUDGED**, *we are chastened of the Lord, that we should not be condemned with the world.* (1 Corinthians 11:23-32)

So that we ourselves glory in you in the churches of God for your *patience and faith* in all your persecutions and tribulations that ye endure: Which is a manifest token of the righteous **JUDGMENT** of God, *that ye may be counted worthy of the kingdom of God, for which ye also suffer:* **Seeing it is a righteous thing with God to recompense tribulation to them that trouble you;** (2 Thessalonians 1:4-6)

I charge thee therefore before God, and the Lord Jesus Christ, who shall **JUDGE** the quick and the dead at his appearing and his kingdom; *Preach the word;* be instant in season, out of season; *reprove, rebuke, exhort* with all long suffering and doctrine. **For the time will come when they will not endure sound doctrine;** but after their own lusts shall they heap to themselves teachers, having itching ears;

And they shall turn away their ears from the truth, and shall be turned unto fables. (2 Timothy 4:1-4)

I have fought a good fight, I have finished my course, I have kept the faith: Henceforth there is laid up for me <u>*a crown of righteousness*</u>, which the Lord, the righteous **JUDGE**, shall give me at that day: and not to me only, but *unto **all** them also that love his appearing.* (2 Timothy 4:7-8)

Some men's <u>sins</u> are open beforehand, going before to **JUDGMENT**; and some men they follow after. Likewise also the <u>*good works*</u> of some are manifest beforehand; and they that are otherwise cannot be hid. (1 Timothy 5:24-25)

Therefore leaving the principles of the doctrine of Christ, *let us go on unto perfection;* not laying again the foundation of repentance from dead works, and of faith toward God, Of the doctrine of baptisms, and of laying on of hands, and of **resurrection of the dead, and of eternal JUDGMENT.** And this will we do, if God permit. (Hebrews 6:1-3)

And as it is appointed unto men once to die, but after this the JUDGMENT: (Hebrews 9:27)

For if we sin *wilfully* after that we have received the knowledge of the truth, there remaineth no more sacrifice for sins, But a certain fearful looking for of JUDGMENT and fiery indignation, which shall devour the adversaries. He that **<u>despised Moses' law</u> died without mercy** under two or three witnesses: **Of how much sorer punishment, suppose ye, shall he be thought worthy, who hath trodden under foot the Son of God, and hath counted the blood of the covenant, wherewith he was sanctified, an unholy thing, and hath done despite unto the Spirit of grace?** For we know him that hath said, **Vengeance belongeth unto me, I will recompense, saith the Lord.** And again, The Lord shall **JUDGE** his people. **It is a fearful thing to fall into the hands of the living God.** (Hebrews 10:26-31)

To the general assembly and church of the firstborn, which are written in heaven, and to **God the JUDGE of all**, and to the spirits of just men made perfect, (Hebrews 12:23)

Marriage is honourable in all, and the bed undefiled: *but* <u>**whoremongers**</u> and <u>**adulterers**</u> **God will JUDGE.** (Hebrews 13:4)

My brethren, have *not* the faith of our Lord Jesus Christ, the Lord of glory, <u>with respect of persons</u>. For if there come unto your assembly a man with a gold ring, in goodly apparel, and there come in also a poor man in vile raiment; And <u>ye have respect to him that weareth the gay clothing</u>, and say unto him, <u>Sit thou here in a good place</u>; and say to the poor, <u>Stand thou there</u>, or <u>sit here under my footstool</u>: **Are ye not then partial in yourselves, and are become JUDGES of evil thoughts?** (James 2:1-4)

For whosoever shall keep the whole law, and yet offend in one point, he is guilty of all. For he that said, Do not commit adultery, said also, Do not kill. Now if thou commit no adultery, yet if thou kill, thou art become a transgressor of the law. So speak ye, and so do, as they that shall be **JUDGED** by the law of liberty. **For he shall have JUDGMENT without mercy, that hath shewed no mercy;** and *mercy rejoiceth against judgment.* What doth it profit, my brethren, *though a man say he hath faith, and have not works? can faith save him?* (James 2:10-14)

Go to now, **ye rich men,** weep and howl for your miseries that shall come upon you. Your riches are corrupted, and your garments are motheaten. Your gold and silver is cankered; and the rust of them shall be **a witness against you, and shall eat your flesh as it were fire.** Ye have heaped treasure together for the last days. Behold, the hire of the labourers who have reaped down your fields, which is of you kept back by fraud, crieth: and the cries of them which have reaped are entered into the ears of the Lord of sabaoth. Ye have lived in pleasure on the earth, and been wanton; ye have nourished your hearts, as in a day of slaughter. Ye have condemned and killed the just; and he doth not resist you. *Be patient therefore, brethren,* unto the coming of the Lord. Behold, *the husbandman waiteth for the precious fruit of the earth, and hath long patience for it,* until he receive the early and latter rain. Be ye also *patient*; *stablish your hearts*: for the coming of the Lord draweth nigh. *Grudge not one against another, brethren*, lest ye be condemned: **behold, the JUDGE standeth before the door.** (James 5:1-9)

As <u>*obedient children*</u>, **not** fashioning yourselves according to the former lusts in your ignorance: But as he which hath called you is holy, *so be ye holy in all manner of conversation;* Because it is written, **Be ye holy; for I am holy.** And if ye call on the Father, who without respect of persons **JUDGETH according to every man's work,** *pass the time of your sojourning here in fear*: (1 Peter 1:14-17)

For even hereunto were ye called: because *Christ also suffered for us, leaving us an example, that ye should follow his steps:* Who did <u>*no sin*</u>, <u>*neither was guile found in his mouth*</u>: Who, when he was reviled, <u>*reviled not again*</u>; when he suffered, he <u>*threatened not*</u>; but **committed himself to him that JUDGETH righteously:** Who his own self bare our sins in his own body on the tree, that ***we, being <u>dead to sins</u>, <u>should live unto righteousness</u>****: by whose stripes ye were healed.* (1 Peter 2:21-24)

Forasmuch then as Christ hath suffered for us in the flesh, arm yourselves likewise with the <u>*same mind*</u>: *for he that hath suffered in the flesh hath ceased from sin; That he no longer should live the rest of his time in the flesh to the lusts of men, but to the will of God.* For the time past of our life may suffice us to have wrought the will of the Gentiles, when we walked in <u>lasciviousness</u>, <u>lusts</u>, <u>excess of wine</u>, <u>revellings</u>, <u>banquetings</u>, and <u>abominable idolatries</u>: Wherein they think it strange that ye run not with them to the same excess of riot, speaking evil of you: **Who shall give account to him that is ready to JUDGE the quick and the dead.** For for this cause was the gospel preached also to them that are dead, that they might be **JUDGED** according to men in the flesh, but *live according to God in the spirit.* (1 Peter 1:4-6)

Beloved, think it not strange concerning the *fiery trial which is to try you,* as though some strange thing happened unto you: But rejoice, inasmuch as *ye are partakers of Christ's sufferings; that, when his glory shall be revealed,* ye may be glad also with exceeding joy. If ye be reproached for the name of Christ, happy are ye; for the spirit of glory and of God resteth upon you: on their part he is evil spoken of, but on your part he is glorified. But let none of you suffer as a <u>murderer</u>, or as a <u>thief</u>, or as an <u>evildoer</u>, or as a <u>busybody</u> in other men's matters. *Yet if any man suffer as a Christian, let him not be ashamed;* but let him glorify God on this behalf. **For the time is come that JUDGMENT** *must begin at the house of God: and if it first begin at <u>us</u>,* **what shall the end be of <u>them</u> that obey** *not* **the gospel of God?** *And if the righteous <u>scarcely</u> be saved,* **where shall the ungodly and the sinner appear?** Wherefore let them that suffer according to the will of God commit the keeping of their souls to him in *well doing,* as unto a faithful Creator. (1 Peter 4:12-19)

But there were **false prophets** also among the people, even as there shall be **false teachers** among you, who privily shall bring in **damnable heresies**, even denying the Lord that bought them, and bring upon themselves swift destruction. And <u>many shall follow their pernicious ways</u>; by reason of whom the way of truth shall be evil spoken of. And through <u>covetousness</u> shall they with feigned words make merchandise of you: **whose JUDGMENT now of a long time lingereth not, and their damnation slumbereth not.** For if God spared not the angels that sinned, but cast them down to hell, and delivered them into chains of darkness, to be reserved unto **JUDGMENT**; And **spared not the old world,** but *saved Noah* the eighth person, a preacher of righteousness, **bringing in the flood upon the world of the ungodly**; And turning the cities of **Sodom and Gomorrha into ashes condemned them with an overthrow,** *making them an ensample* unto those that after should live ungodly; And *delivered just Lot*, vexed with the filthy conversation of the wicked: (For that righteous man dwelling among them, in seeing and hearing, vexed his righteous soul from day to day with their unlawful deeds;) The Lord knoweth how to deliver the godly out of temptations, and to **reserve the unjust unto the day of JUDGMENT to be punished:** (2 Peter 2:1-9)

But the heavens and the earth, which are now, by the same word are kept in store, **reserved unto fire against the day of JUDGMENT and perdition of ungodly men.** (2 Peter 3:7)

And <u>the angels</u> which kept not their first estate, but left their own habitation, he hath reserved in everlasting chains under darkness unto the **JUDGMENT of the great day.** (Jude 1:6)

And *Enoch* also, the seventh from Adam, prophesied of these, saying, Behold, the Lord cometh with ten thousands of his saints, **To execute JUDGMENT upon** *all*, **and to convince** *all* **that are ungodly among them of** *all* **their ungodly deeds which they have ungodly committed, and of** *all* **their hard speeches which ungodly sinners have spoken against him.** These are murmurers, complainers, walking after their own lusts; and their mouth speaketh great swelling words, having men's persons in admiration because of advantage. But, beloved, remember ye the words which were spoken before of the apostles of our Lord Jesus Christ; How that they told you there should be mockers in the last time, who should walk after their own ungodly lusts. **These be they who** *separate themselves,* **sensual, having not the Spirit.** (Jude 1:14-19)

And when he had opened the fifth seal, I saw under the altar the souls of *them that were slain for the word of God, and for the testimony which they held:* And they cried with a loud voice, saying, **How long, O Lord, holy and true, dost thou not JUDGE and** *avenge our blood* **on them that dwell on the earth?** (Revelation 6:9-10)

And the *four and twenty elders*, which sat before God on their seats, fell upon their faces, and worshipped God, Saying, *We give thee thanks, O L*ORD *God Almighty, which art, and wast, and art to* *come; because thou hast taken to thee thy great power, and hast reigned.* **And the nations were angry, and thy wrath is come, and the time of the dead, that they should be JUDGED,** and that thou shouldest give *reward unto thy servants* <u>the prophets</u>, and to <u>the saints</u>, and <u>them that fear thy name</u>, small and great; and **shouldest destroy them which destroy the earth.** (Revelation 11:16-18)

And I heard a great voice out of the temple saying to the <u>seven angels</u>, **Go your ways, and pour out the vials of the wrath of God upon the earth.** And the *<u>first</u>* went, and poured out his vial upon the <u>earth</u>; and there fell a noisome and *grievous sore* upon the men which had **the mark of the beast**, and upon them which **worshipped his image.** And the *second angel* poured out his vial upon the <u>sea</u>; and it became as the *blood* of a dead man: and every living soul died in the sea. And the *third angel* poured out his vial upon the <u>rivers and fountains of waters</u>; and they became *blood*. And I heard the angel of the waters say, **Thou art righteous, O Lord, which art, and wast, and shalt be, because thou hast JUDGED thus. For they have shed the blood of saints and prophets, and thou hast given them blood to drink; for they are worthy**. And I heard another out of the altar say, Even so, Lord God Almighty, true and righteous are thy **JUDGMENTS**. (Revelation 6:1-7)

And I saw *another angel* fly in the midst of heaven, having the ***everlasting gospel*** to preach unto them that dwell on the earth, and to every nation, and kindred, and tongue, and people, Saying with a loud voice, **Fear God, and give glory to him; for the hour of his JUDGMENT is come: and worship him that made heaven, and earth, and the sea, and the fountains of waters.** And there followed another angel, saying, **Babylon is fallen, is fallen, that great city, because she made all nations drink of the wine of the wrath of her fornication.** And the <u>*third angel*</u> followed them, saying with a loud voice, **If any man <u>worship</u> the beast and his image, and receive his <u>mark</u> in his forehead, or in his hand, The same shall drink of the wine of the *wrath of God*, which is poured out without mixture into the cup of his indignation;** *and* **he shall be tormented with fire and brimstone in the presence of the holy angels, and in the presence of the Lamb:** And the smoke of their torment ascendeth up for ever and ever: and **they have no rest day nor night, who worship the beast and his image, and whosoever receiveth** *the mark* **of his name.** (Revelation 14:6-11)

And I saw another sign in heaven, great and marvellous, seven angels having the <u>seven last plagues</u>; **for in them is filled up the** *wrath* **of God.** And I saw as it were a <u>*sea of glass*</u> mingled with fire: and them that had gotten the ***victory*** *over the beast,* and over his image, and over *his mark*, and over *the number of his name*, stand on the sea of glass, having the harps of God. And they sing the song of Moses the servant of God, and the song of the Lamb, saying, *Great and marvellous are thy works, Lord God Almighty; just and true are thy ways, thou King of saints. Who shall not fear thee, O Lord, and glorify thy name? for thou only art holy: for all nations shall come and worship before* thee; for thy **JUDGMENTS** are made manifest. (Revelation 15:1-4)

And I heard a *great voice* out of the temple saying to the seven angels, **Go your ways, and pour out the vials of the wrath of God upon the earth.** And the *first* went, and poured out his vial upon the earth; and there fell a noisome and grievous *sore* upon the men which had the **mark of the beast**, and upon them which **worshipped his image.** And the *second angel* poured out his vial upon the sea; and it became as the *blood* of a dead man: and every living soul died in the sea. And the *third angel* poured out his vial upon the rivers and fountains of waters; and they became *blood*. And I heard the angel of the waters say, **Thou art righteous, O Lord, which art, and wast, and shalt be, because thou hast judged thus. For they have shed the blood of saints and prophets, and thou hast given them blood to drink; for they are worthy.** And I heard another out of the altar say, Even so, Lord God Almighty, true and righteous are thy **JUDGMENTS.** (Revelation 16:1-7)

And there came one of the *seven angels* which had the *seven vials*, and talked with me, saying unto me, Come hither; I will shew unto thee the **JUDGMENT** of **the great whore** that sitteth upon many waters: With whom **the kings** of the earth have committed fornication, and the inhabitants of the earth have been made drunk with the wine of her fornication. So he carried me away in the spirit into the wilderness: and I saw **a woman** sit upon a **scarlet coloured beast**, full of names of blasphemy, having <u>seven heads and ten horns</u>. And the woman was <u>arrayed in purple</u> *and* <u>scarlet colour</u>, and <u>decked with gold</u> *and* <u>precious stones</u> *and* <u>pearls</u>, having a <u>golden cup</u> in her hand <u>full of abominations</u> *and* <u>filthiness of her fornication</u>: And upon her forehead was a name written, **MYSTERY, BABYLON THE GREAT, THE MOTHER OF HARLOTS AND ABOMINATIONS OF THE EARTH.** And I saw **the woman drunken with the blood of the saints, and with the blood of the martyrs of Jesus:** and when I saw her, I wondered with great admiration. (Revelation 17:1-6)

And after these things I saw *<u>another angel</u>* come down from heaven, having great power; and the earth was lightened with his glory. And he cried mightily with a strong voice, saying, **Babylon the great is fallen, is fallen,** and is become the <u>habitation of devils,</u> and the hold of <u>every foul spirit,</u> and a cage of <u>every unclean and hateful bird.</u> **For** *all* **nations have drunk of the wine of the wrath of her** <u>**fornication**</u>**, and the kings** of the earth have committed <u>fornication with her</u>, and the **merchants** of the earth are <u>waxed rich</u> through the abundance of her delicacies. And I heard another voice from heaven, saying, *Come out of her, <u>my people</u>, that ye be not partakers of her sins, and that ye receive not of her plagues.* For her sins have reached unto heaven, and God hath remembered her iniquities. **Reward her even as she rewarded you, and double unto her double according to her works: in the cup which she hath filled fill to her double.** How much she hath <u>glorified herself</u>, and <u>lived deliciously</u>, so much **torment and sorrow give her:** for she saith in her heart, **I sit a queen,** *and* **am no widow,** and shall see no sorrow. **Therefore shall her plagues come in one day, death, and mourning, and famine; and she shall be utterly burned with fire: for strong is the Lord God who JUDGETH her.** And **the kings** of the earth, who have committed <u>fornication</u> and <u>lived deliciously</u> with her, shall bewail her, and lament for her, when they shall see the smoke of her burning, Standing afar off for the fear of her torment, saying, **Alas, alas that great city Babylon, that mighty city! for in one hour is thy JUDGMENT come.** And **the merchants** of the earth shall weep and mourn over her; for no man buyeth their merchandise any more: (Revelation 18:1-11)

For true and righteous are his **JUDGMENTS: for he hath judged <u>the great whore</u>, which did corrupt the earth with her <u>fornication</u>,** and hath avenged the blood of his servants at her hand. And again they said, *Alleluia* And her smoke rose up for ever and ever. (Revelation 19:2-3)

And I saw heaven opened, and behold a *<u>white horse</u>*; and he that sat upon him was called ***Faithful and True,*** and ***in righteousness he doth*** **JUDGE *and make war.*** His *<u>eyes</u>* were as a flame of fire, and on his *<u>head</u>* were many crowns; and he had a *<u>name</u>* written, that no man knew, but he himself. And he was clothed with *<u>a vesture dipped in blood</u>*: and *<u>his name</u>* is called ***The Word of God.*** And the armies which were in heaven followed him upon white horses, clothed in fine linen, white and clean. And out of his mouth goeth a sharp sword, that with it he should *smite the nations: and he shall rule them with a rod of iron: and he treadeth the winepress of the fierceness and wrath of Almighty God.* And he hath on his vesture and on his thigh a name written, **KING OF KINGS, AND LORD OF LORDS.** (Revelation 19:11-16)

And I saw <u>*an angel*</u> come down from heaven, having the key of the bottomless pit and a great chain in his hand. And he laid hold on **the dragon**, that **old serpent**, which is **the Devil**, and **Satan**, and bound him a thousand years. And cast him into the bottomless pit, and shut him up, and set a seal upon him, **that he should deceive the nations no more,** till the thousand years should be fulfilled: and after that he must be loosed a little season. And I saw thrones, and they sat upon them, and **JUDGMENT** was given unto them: and *I saw the souls of them that were beheaded for the witness of Jesus, and for the word of God, and which had not worshipped the beast, neither his image, neither had received his mark upon their foreheads, or in their hands; and they lived and reigned with Christ a thousand years.* But the rest of the dead lived not again until the thousand years were finished. This is the first resurrection. (Revelation 20:1-5)

And I saw a *great white throne*, and him that sat on it, from whose face the earth and the heaven fled away; and there was found no place for them. And *I saw the dead, small and great, stand before God;* and the books were opened: and another book was opened, which is the book of life: and **the dead were JUDGED out of those things which were written in**

the books, *according to their works.* And the sea gave up the dead which were in it; and death and hell delivered up the dead which were in them: and **they were JUDGED every man** *according to their works.* And death and hell were cast into the lake of fire. This is the second death. **And whosoever was not found written in the book of life was cast into the lake of fire.** (Revelation 20:11-15)

Chapter 29

PERDITION

And **in nothing terrified by your adversaries:** which is to them an evident token of **PERDITION,** but to you of salvation, and that of God. For unto you it is given in the behalf of Christ, *not only to believe on him, but also to suffer for his sake;* (Phillipians 1:28-29)

Now we beseech you, brethren, by the coming of our Lord Jesus Christ, and by our gathering together unto him, That ye be not soon shaken in mind, or be troubled, neither by spirit, nor by word, nor by letter as from us, as that the day of Christ is at hand. <u>**Let no man *deceive* you by any means:**</u> **for that day shall not come, except there come a falling away first, and that <u>man of sin</u> be revealed, the son of PERDITION; Who opposeth and exalteth himself above all that is called God, or that is worshipped; so that he as God sitteth in the temple of God, <u>shewing himself that he is God</u>.** (2 Thessalonians 2:1-4)

But godliness with contentment is great gain. For we brought nothing into this world, and it is certain we can carry nothing out. And having food and raiment let us be therewith content. But **they that will be *rich* fall into temptation and a snare, and into many foolish and hurtful lusts, which drown men in destruction and PERDITION. For the *love of money* is the <u>root of all evil</u>:** which while some coveted after, they have erred from the faith, and pierced themselves through with many sorrows.

*But thou, O man of God, **flee** these things;* and follow after *righteousness, godliness, faith, love, patience, meekness.* ***Fight** the good fight of faith,* lay hold on eternal life, whereunto thou art also called, and hast professed a good profession before many witnesses. (1 Timothy 6:6-12)

Now the just shall live by faith: *but* **if any man** *draw back***, my soul shall have *no* pleasure in him.** But we are not of them who *draw back* unto **PERDITION**; but of them that believe to the saving of the soul. (Hebrews 10:38-39)

Knowing this first, that there shall come in the last days scoffers, walking after their own lusts, And saying, *Where* is the promise of his coming? for since the fathers fell asleep, all things continue as they were from the beginning of the creation. For this they **willingly are ignorant** of, that by the word of God the heavens were of old, and the earth standing out of the water and in the water: Whereby the world that then was, being overflowed with water, perished: But **the heavens and the earth,** which are now, by the same word are kept in store, **reserved unto fire against the day of judgment and PERDITION of ungodly men.** But, beloved, be not ignorant of this one thing, *that one day is with the Lord as a thousand years, and a thousand years as one day. The Lord is not slack concerning his promise,* as some men count slackness; but is *longsuffering* to us-ward, not willing that any should perish, but **that all should come to *repentance*.** (2 Peter 3:3-9)

And there came one of the _seven angels_ which had the seven vials, and talked with me, saying unto me, Come hither; I will shew unto thee **the judgment of the great whore** that sitteth upon many waters: With whom the kings of the earth have committed fornication, and **the inhabitants** of the earth have been made drunk with the wine of her fornication. So he carried me away in the spirit into the wilderness: and I saw **a woman** sit upon a **scarlet coloured beast**, full of names of blasphemy, having seven heads and ten horns. And **the woman was arrayed in purple and scarlet colour, and decked with gold and precious stones and pearls, having a golden cup in her hand full of abominations and filthiness of her _fornication_**: And upon her forehead was a name written, **MYSTERY, BABYLON THE GREAT, THE MOTHER OF HARLOTS AND ABOMINATIONS OF THE EARTH.** And I saw the woman drunken with the blood of the saints, and with the blood of the martyrs of Jesus: and when I saw her, I wondered with great admiration. And the angel said unto me, Wherefore didst thou marvel? I will tell thee the mystery of **the woman**, and of **the beast** that carrieth her, which hath the seven heads and ten horns. **The beast** that thou sawest was, and is not; and **shall ascend out of the bottomless pit, and go into PERDITION**: and they that dwell on the earth shall wonder, **whose names were not written in the book of life** from the foundation of the world, when they behold **the beast that was, and is not, and yet is**. And here is the mind which hath wisdom. The seven heads are seven mountains, on which **the woman sitteth**. And there are **seven kings:** five are fallen, and one is, and the other is not yet come; and when he cometh, he must continue a short space. And **the beast** that was, and is not, even he is the eighth, and is of the seven, and goeth into **PERDITION**. And the **ten horns** which thou sawest are **ten kings,** which have received no kingdom as yet; but **receive power as kings one hour with the beast.** <u>**These have one mind, and shall give their power and strength unto the beast.**</u> **These shall make war with the Lamb,** *and the Lamb shall overcome them: for he is Lord of lords, and King of kings: and they that are with him are called, and chosen, and faithful.* (Revelation 17:1-14)

Chapter 30

BEWARE

BEWARE of <u>false prophets</u>, which come to you in <u>sheep's clothing</u>, but inwardly they are <u>ravening wolves</u>. Ye shall know them by their *fruits.* Do men gather grapes of thorns, or figs of thistles? Even so every *good tree* bringeth forth <u>good fruit</u>; but a *corrupt tree* bringeth forth <u>evil fruit</u>. A good tree cannot bring forth evil fruit, neither can a corrupt tree bring forth good fruit. **Every tree that bringeth not forth** *good* **fruit is hewn down, and cast into the fire.** Wherefore by their *fruits* ye shall know them. **Not every one that saith unto me, Lord, Lord, shall enter into the kingdom of heaven; but he that** *<u>doeth</u>* **the will of my Father which is in heaven.** *<u>Many</u>* will say to me in that day, Lord, Lord, have we not prophesied in thy name? and in thy name have cast out devils? and in thy name done many wonderful works? And then will I profess unto them, <u>**I never knew you: depart from me, ye that work iniquity.**</u> (Matthew 7:15-23)

How is it that ye do not understand that I spake it not to you concerning bread, that ye should **BEWARE** of the leaven of the Pharisees and of the Sadducees? Then understood they how that he bade them not **BEWARE** of the leaven of bread, but of **the doctrine** of the Pharisees and of the Sadducees. (Matthew 16:11-12)

And he charged them, saying, **Take heed, BEWARE** of the leaven of the Pharisees, and of the leaven of Herod. (Mark 8:15)

And he said unto them in his doctrine, **BEWARE of the scribes,** which love to go in <u>long clothing</u>, and <u>love salutations in the marketplaces,</u> And the <u>chief seats in the synagogues</u>, and the <u>uppermost rooms at feasts</u>: Which <u>devour widows' houses</u>, and <u>for a pretence make long prayers</u>: **these shall receive greater damnation.** (Mark 12:38-40)

In the mean time, when there were gathered together an innumerable multitude of people, insomuch that they trode one upon another, he began to say unto his disciples first of all, **BEWARE** ye of the leaven of the Pharisees, which is <u>hypocrisy</u>. **For there is nothing covered, that shall not be revealed; neither hid, that shall not be known.** Therefore whatsoever ye have spoken in darkness shall be heard in the light; and that which ye have spoken in the ear in closets shall be proclaimed upon the housetops. And I say unto you my friends, **Be not afraid of them that kill the body,** and after that have no more that they can do. But I will forewarn you whom ye shall fear: *Fear him, which after he hath killed hath power to cast into hell; yea, I say unto you, Fear him.* Are not five sparrows sold for two farthings, and not one of them is forgotten before God? But even the very hairs of your head are all numbered. Fear not therefore: ye are of more value than many sparrows. Also I say unto you, <u>Whosoever shall confess me before men, him shall the Son of man also confess before the</u>

angels of God: *But* he that denieth me before men shall be denied before the angels of God. And whosoever shall speak a word against the Son of man, it shall be forgiven him: *but* **unto him that blasphemeth against the Holy Ghost it shall not be forgiven.** And when they bring you unto the synagogues, and unto magistrates, and powers, take ye no thought how or what thing ye shall answer, or what ye shall say: For the Holy Ghost shall teach you in the same hour what ye ought to say. And one of the company said unto him, Master, speak to my brother, that he divide the inheritance with me. And he said unto him, Man, who made me a judge or a divider over you? And he said unto them, **Take heed,** and **BEWARE** of covetousness: for a man's life consisteth *not* in the abundance of the things which he possesseth. (Luke 12:1-15)

Then in the audience of all the people he said unto his disciples, **BEWARE of the scribes**, which desire to walk in long robes, and love greetings in the markets, and the highest seats in the synagogues, and the chief rooms at feasts; Which devour widows' houses, and for a shew make long prayers: **the same shall receive greater damnation.** (Luke 20:45-47)

But he, whom God raised again, saw no corruption. Be it known unto you therefore, men and brethren, that through this man is preached unto you the forgiveness of sins: And by him all that believe are justified from all things, from which ye could not be justified by the law of Moses. **BEWARE** therefore, lest that come upon you, which is spoken of in the prophets; **Behold, ye despisers, and wonder, and perish:** for I work a work in your days, a work which ye shall in no wise believe, though a man declare it unto you. (Acts 13:37-41)

BEWARE of dogs, BEWARE of evil workers, BEWARE of the concision. (Philippians 3:2)

As ye have therefore received Christ Jesus the Lord, so walk ye in him: Rooted and built up in him, and stablished in the faith, as ye have been taught, abounding therein with thanksgiving. **BEWARE lest any man spoil you through philosophy and vain deceit, after the tradition of men, after the rudiments of the world, and *not* after Christ.** For in him dwelleth all the fulness of the Godhead bodily. And ye are complete in him, which is the head of all principality and power: (Colossians 2:6-10)

Ye therefore, beloved, seeing ye know these things before, **BEWARE lest ye also, being led away with the error of the wicked, fall from your own stedfastness.** (2 Peter 3:17)

Chapter 31

REPENT

In those days came John the Baptist, preaching in the wilderness of Judaea, And saying, **REPENT** ye: for the kingdom of heaven is at hand. For this is he that was spoken of by the prophet Esaias, saying, The voice of one crying in the wilderness, *Prepare ye the way of the Lord, make his paths straight*. And the same John had his raiment of camel's hair, and a leathern girdle about his loins; and his meat was locusts and wild honey. Then went out to him Jerusalem, and all Judaea, and all the region round about Jordan, and were baptized of him in Jordan, confessing their sins. But when he saw many of the Pharisees and Sadducees come to his baptism, he said unto them, O generation of vipers, who hath warned you to flee from the wrath to come? *Bring forth therefore fruits meet for* **REPENTANCE**: (Matthew 3:1-8)

The people which sat in darkness saw great light; and to them which sat in the region and shadow of death *light is sprung up.* From that time Jesus began to preach, and to say, **REPENT**: for the kingdom of heaven is at hand. (Matthew 4:16-18)

But when Jesus heard that, he said unto them, They that be whole need not a physician, but they that are sick. But go ye and learn what that meaneth, I will have mercy, and not sacrifice: for *I am not come to call the righteous, but sinners to* **REPENTANCE**. (Matthew 9:12-13)

The beginning of the gospel of Jesus Christ, the Son of God; As it is written in the prophets, Behold, I send my messenger before thy face, which shall prepare thy way before thee. The voice of one crying in the wilderness, ***Prepare ye the way of the Lord, make his paths straight.*** John did baptize in the wilderness, and preach the baptism of **REPENTANCE** *for the remission of sins.* And there went out unto him all the land of Judaea, and they of Jerusalem, and were all baptized of him in the river of Jordan, *confessing their sins.* (Mark 1:1-5)

Now after that John was put in prison, Jesus came into Galilee, preaching the gospel of the kingdom of God, And saying, The time is fulfilled, and the kingdom of God is at hand: **REPENT** *ye, and believe the gospel.* (Mark 1:14-15)

And it came to pass, that, as Jesus sat at meat in his house, many publicans and sinners sat also together with Jesus and his disciples: for there were many, and they followed him. And when the scribes and Pharisees saw him eat with publicans and sinners, they said unto his disciples, How is it that he eateth and drinketh with publicans and sinners? When Jesus heard it, he saith unto them, They that are whole have no need of the physician, but they that are sick: *I came not to call the righteous, but sinners to* **REPENTANCE**. (Mark 2:15-17)

And he called unto him the twelve, and began to send them forth by two and two; and gave them *power over unclean spirits;* And commanded them that they should take nothing for their journey, save a staff only; no scrip, no bread, no money in their purse: But be shod with sandals; and not put on two coats. And he said unto them, In what place soever ye enter into an house, there abide till ye depart from that place. And whosoever shall not receive you, nor hear you, when ye depart thence, shake off the dust under your feet for a testimony against them. Verily I say unto you, It shall be more tolerable for Sodom and Gomorrha in the day of judgment, than for that city. **And they went out, and preached that men should REPENT.** *And they cast out many devils, and anointed with oil many that were sick, and healed them.* (Mark 6:7-13)

Now in the fifteenth year of the reign of Tiberius Caesar, Pontius Pilate being governor of Judaea, and Herod being tetrarch of Galilee, and his brother Philip tetrarch of Ituraea and of the region of Trachonitis, and Lysanias the tetrarch of Abilene, Annas and Caiaphas being the high priests, the word of God came unto John the son of Zacharias in the wilderness. And he came into all the country about Jordan, *preaching the baptism of* **REPENTANCE** *for the remission of sins;* As it is written in the book of the words of Esaias the prophet, saying, The voice of one crying in the wilderness, *Prepare ye the way of the Lord, make his paths straight. Every valley shall be filled, and every mountain and hill shall be brought low; and the crooked shall be made straight, and the rough* *ways shall be made smooth; And all flesh shall see the salvation of God.* Then said he to the multitude that came forth to be baptized of him, O generation of vipers, who hath warned you to flee from the wrath to come? **Bring forth therefore fruits worthy of REPENTANCE**, and begin not to say within yourselves, We have Abraham to our father: for I say unto you, That God is able of these stones to raise up children unto Abraham. And now also the axe is laid unto the root of the trees: every tree therefore which bringeth not forth good fruit is hewn down, and cast into the fire. (Luke 3:1-9)

And Jesus answering said unto them, They that are whole need not a physician; but they that are sick. *I came not to call the righteous, but sinners to* **REPENTANCE**. (Luke 5:31-32)

I tell you, Nay: but, *except ye* **REPENT**, ye shall all likewise perish. (Luke 13:3)

I tell you, Nay: but, *except ye* **REPENT**, ye shall all likewise perish. (Luke 13:5)

I say unto you, that likewise joy shall be in heaven over one sinner that **REPENTETH**, more than over ninety and nine just persons, which need no **REPENTANCE**. (Luke 15:7)

Likewise, I say unto you, *there is joy in the presence of the angels of God over one sinner that* **REPENTETH**. (Luke 15:10)

And he said unto them, These are the words which I spake unto you, while I was yet with you, that all things must be fulfilled, which were written in the law of Moses, and in the prophets, and in the psalms, concerning me. Then opened he their understanding, that they might understand the scriptures, And said unto them, Thus it is written, and thus it behooved Christ to suffer, and to rise from the dead the third day: And that **REPENTANCE** *and remission of sins should be preached in his name among all nations, beginning at Jerusalem.* (Luke 24:44-47)

Therefore let all the house of Israel know assuredly, that God hath made the same Jesus, whom ye have crucified, both Lord and Christ. Now when they heard this, they were pricked in their heart, and said unto Peter and to the rest of the apostles, Men and brethren, what shall we do? Then Peter said unto them, **REPENT**, *and be baptized every one of you in the name of Jesus Christ for the remission of sins, and ye shall receive the gift of the Holy Ghost.* For the promise is unto you, and to your children, and to all that are afar off, even as many as the Lord our God shall call. And with many other words did he testify and exhort, saying, *Save yourselves from this untoward generation.* (Acts 2:36-40)

REPENT *ye therefore, and be converted, that your sins may be blotted out,* when the times of refreshing shall come from the presence of the Lord. (Acts 3:19)

Him hath God exalted with his right hand to be a Prince and a Saviour, for to give **REPENTANCE** to Israel, and *forgiveness of sins.* (Acts 5:31)

REPENT *therefore of this thy wickedness,* and pray God, if perhaps the thought of thine heart may be forgiven thee. (Acts 8:22)

When they heard these things, they held their peace, and glorified God, saying, Then hath God also to the Gentiles granted **REPENTANCE** *unto life.* (Acts 11:18)

And afterward they desired a king: and God gave unto them Saul the son of Cis, a man of the tribe of Benjamin, by the space of forty years. And when he had removed him, he raised up unto them David to be their king; to whom also he gave their testimony, and said, I have found David the son of Jesse, *a man after mine own heart,* **which shall fulfil all my will.** Of this man's seed hath God according to his promise raised unto Israel a Saviour, Jesus: When *John had first preached before his coming the baptism of* **REPENTANCE** to all the people of Israel. (Acts 13:21-24)

Forasmuch then as we are the offspring of God, we ought not to think that the Godhead is like unto gold, or silver, or stone, graven by art and man's device. And the times of this ignorance God winked at; ***but now commandeth all men every where to* REPENT**: Because he hath appointed a day, in the which he will judge the world in righteousness by that man whom he hath ordained; whereof he hath given assurance unto all men, in that he hath raised him from the dead. (Acts 17:29-31)

Then said Paul, John verily baptized with the ***baptism of* REPENTANCE**, saying unto the people, that *they should believe on him which should come after him, that is, on Christ Jesus.* (Acts 19:4)

Testifying both to the Jews, and also to the Greeks, **REPENTANCE *toward God,*** and faith toward our Lord Jesus Christ. (Acts 20:21)

But shewed first unto them of Damascus, and at Jerusalem, and throughout all the coasts of Judaea, and then to the Gentiles, that they should **REPENT *and turn to God, and do works meet for* REPENTANCE**. (Acts 26:20)

Or despisest thou the riches of his goodness and forbearance and longsuffering; not knowing that ***the goodness of God leadeth thee to* REPENTANCE**? (Romans 2:4)

For though I made you sorry with a letter, I do not **REPENT**, though I did **REPENT**: for I perceive that the same epistle hath made you sorry, though it were but for a season. Now I rejoice, not that ye were made sorry, but that ye sorrowed to **REPENTANCE**: for ye were made sorry after a godly manner, that ye might receive damage by us in nothing. *For godly sorrow worketh* **REPENTANCE** *to salvation* not to be **REPENTED** of: but the sorrow of the world worketh death. (2 Corinthians 7:8-10)

And the servant of the Lord must not strive; but be gentle unto all men, apt to teach, patient, In meekness instructing those that oppose themselves; if God peradventure will give them **REPENTANCE** *to the acknowledging of the truth; And that they may recover themselves out of the snare of the devil,* who are taken captive by him at his will. (2 Timothy 2:24-26)

But the heavens and the earth, which are now, by the same word are kept in store, reserved unto fire against the day of judgment and perdition of ungodly men. But, beloved, be not ignorant of this one thing, that one day is with the Lord as a thousand years, and a thousand years as one day. The Lord is not slack concerning his promise, as some men count slackness; but is *longsuffering to us-ward, not willing that any should perish, but that all should come to* **REPENTANCE**. (2 Peter 3:7-9)

Unto the angel of the church of Ephesus write; These things saith he that holdeth the seven stars in his right hand, who walketh in the midst of the seven golden candlesticks; I know thy works, and thy labour, and thy patience, and how thou canst not bear them which are evil: and thou hast tried them which say they are apostles, and are not, and hast found them liars: And hast borne, and hast patience, and for my name's sake hast laboured, and hast not fainted. Nevertheless I have somewhat against thee, because thou hast left thy first love. ***Remember therefore from whence thou art fallen, and* REPENT**, and do the first works; or else I will come unto thee quickly, and will remove thy candlestick out of his place, *except thou* **REPENT**. (Revelation 2:1-5)

And to the angel of the church in Pergamos write; These things saith he which hath the sharp sword with two edges; I know thy works, and where thou dwellest, even where Satan's seat is: and *thou holdest fast my name, and hast not denied my faith*, even in those days wherein Antipas was my faithful martyr, who was slain among you, where Satan dwelleth. *But* I have a few things against thee, because thou hast there them that hold the doctrine of Balaam, who taught Balac to cast a stumblingblock before the children of Israel, to eat things sacrificed unto idols, *and* to commit fornication. So hast thou also them that hold the doctrine of the Nicolaitanes, which thing I hate. **REPENT; or else** I will come unto thee quickly, and will fight against them with the sword of my mouth. *He that hath an ear, let him hear* what the Spirit saith unto the churches; To him that **overcometh** will I give to eat of the hidden manna, and will give him a white stone, and in the stone a new name written, which no man knoweth saving he that receiveth it. (Revelation 2:12-17)

And unto the angel of the church in Thyatira write; These things saith the Son of God, who hath his eyes like unto a flame of fire, and his feet are like fine brass; I know thy works, and charity, and service, and faith, and thy patience, and thy works; and the last to be more than the first. *Notwithstanding* I have a few things against thee, because thou sufferest that woman Jezebel, which *calleth* herself a prophetess, to teach and to seduce my servants to commit fornication, *and* to eat things sacrificed unto idols. And I gave her space to **REPENT** of her fornication; and **she REPENTED not.** Behold, I will cast her into a bed, and them that commit adultery with her into great tribulation, *except they* **REPENT** *of their deeds.* And I will kill her children with death; and all the churches shall know that *I am he which searcheth the reins and hearts: and I will give unto every one of you according to your works.* But unto you I say, and unto the rest in Thyatira, as many as have *not* this doctrine, and which have *not* known the depths of Satan, as they speak; I will put upon you none other burden. But that which ye have already hold fast till I come. And he that *overcometh, and keepeth my works unto the end, to him will I give power over the nations:* And he shall rule them with a rod of iron; as the vessels of a potter shall they be broken to shivers: even as I received of my Father. And I will give him the morning star. *He that hath an ear, let him hear* what the Spirit saith unto the churches. (Revelation 2:18-29)

And unto the angel of the church in Sardis write; These things saith he that hath the seven Spirits of

God, and the seven stars; I know thy works, that thou hast a name that thou livest, and art dead. Be watchful, and strengthen the things which remain, that are ready to die: for I have NOT found thy works perfect before God. **Remember therefore how thou hast received and heard, and hold fast, and REPENT.** If therefore thou shalt *not* watch, I will come on thee as a thief, and thou shalt not know what hour I will come upon thee. Thou hast a few names even in <u>Sardis</u> which have *not defiled* their garments; and they shall walk with me in white: *for they are worthy.* He that *overcometh,* the same shall be clothed in white raiment; and I will *not* blot out his name out of the book of life, but I will confess his name before my Father, and before his angels. *He that hath an ear, let him hear* what the Spirit saith unto the churches. (Revelation 3:1-6)

And unto the angel of the <u>church of the Laodiceans</u> write; These things saith the Amen, the faithful and true witness, the beginning of the creation of God; *I know thy works, that thou art neither cold nor hot: I would thou wert cold or hot. So then because thou art lukewarm, and neither cold nor hot, I will spue thee out of my mouth.* Because thou sayest, <u>I am rich</u>, and increased with goods, and have need of nothing; and knowest not that thou art wretched, and miserable, and poor, and blind, and naked: I counsel thee to buy of me gold tried in the fire, that thou mayest be rich; and white raiment, that thou mayest be clothed, and that the shame of thy nakedness do not appear; and anoint thine eyes with eyesalve, that thou mayest see. *As many as I love, I rebuke and chasten:* be zealous therefore, and **REPENT**. *Behold, I stand at the door, and knock: if any man hear my voice, and open the door, I will come in to him, and will sup with him, and he with me.* To him that *overcometh* will I grant to sit with me in my throne, even as I also overcame, and am set down with my Father in his throne. *He that hath an ear, let him hear* what the Spirit saith unto the churches. (Revelation 3:14-22)

And thus I saw the *horses* in the vision, and them that sat on them, having breastplates of fire, and of jacinth, and brimstone: and the heads of the horses were as the heads of lions; and out of their mouths issued fire and smoke and brimstone. By these three was the third part of men killed, by the fire, and by the smoke, and by the brimstone, which issued out of their mouths. For their power is in their mouth, and in their tails: for their tails were like unto serpents, and had heads, and with them they do hurt. **And the rest of the men which were not killed by these plagues yet REPENTED NOT of the works of their hands, that they should not worship devils, and idols of gold, and silver, and brass, and stone, and of wood: which neither can see, nor hear, nor walk: NEITHER REPENTED THEY of their murders, nor of their sorceries, nor of their fornication, nor of their thefts.** (Revelation 9:17-21)

And the fourth angel poured out his vial upon the sun; and power was given unto him to scorch men with fire. And men were scorched with great heat, and blasphemed the name of God, which hath power over these plagues: and they **REPENTED NOT to give him glory.** And the <u>fifth angel</u> poured out his vial upon the seat of the beast; and his kingdom was full of darkness; and they gnawed their tongues for pain, And **blasphemed the God of heaven because of their pains and their sores,** *and* **REPENTED not of their deeds.** (Revelation 16:8-11)

Chapter 32

STRIVE

Then said one unto him, Lord, are there few that be saved? And he said unto them, **STRIVE** to enter in at the strait gate: **for many, I say unto you, will seek to enter in, and shall not be able.** (Luke 13:23-24)

Know ye not that they which run in a race run all, but one receiveth the prize? *So run, that ye may obtain.* And every man that **STRIVETH** for the mastery is temperate in all things. Now they do it to obtain a corruptible crown; but we an incorruptible. (1 Corinthians 9:24-25)

Chapter 33

TURN

Yea, and all the prophets from Samuel and those that follow after, as many as have spoken, have likewise foretold of these days. Ye are the children of the prophets, and of the covenant which God made with our fathers, saying unto Abraham, And in thy seed shall all the kindreds of the earth be blessed. Unto you first God, having raised up his Son Jesus, sent him to bless you, in **TURNING** *away every one of you from his iniquities.* (Acts 3:24-26)

And saying, Sirs, why do ye these things? We also are men of like passions with you, and preach unto you that *ye should* **TURN** *from these vanities unto the living God,* which made heaven, and earth, and the sea, and all things that are therein: (Acts 14:15)

And when we were all fallen to the earth, I heard a voice speaking unto me, and saying in the Hebrew tongue, Saul, Saul, why persecutest thou me? it is hard for thee to kick against the pricks. And I said, Who art thou, Lord? And he said, I am Jesus whom thou persecutest. But rise, and stand upon thy feet: for I have appeared unto thee for this purpose, to make thee a minister and a witness both of these things which thou hast seen, and of those things in the which I will appear unto thee; Delivering thee from the people, and from the Gentiles, unto whom now I send thee, *To open their eyes, and to* **TURN** *them from darkness to light, and from the power of Satan unto God, that they may receive forgiveness of sins,* and inheritance among them which are sanctified by faith that is in me. (Acts 26:14)

But shewed first unto them of Damascus, and at Jerusalem, and throughout all the coasts of Judaea, and then to the Gentiles, that *they should repent and* **TURN** *to God, and do works meet for repentance.* (Acts 26:20)

And so all Israel shall be saved: as it is written, There shall come out of Sion the Deliverer, and shall **TURN** *away ungodliness* from Jacob: For this is my covenant unto them, when I shall take away their sins. (Romans 11:26-27)

And not as Moses, which put a veil over his face, that the children of Israel could not stedfastly look to the end of that which is abolished: But their minds were blinded: for until this day remaineth the same vail untaken away in the reading of the old testament; *which vail is done away in Christ.* <u>But even unto this day, when Moses is read, the vail is upon their heart.</u> *Nevertheless when it shall* **TURN** *to the Lord, the vail shall be taken away.* (2 Corinthians 13-16)

For they themselves shew of us what manner of entering in we had unto you, and how ye **TURNED** *to God from idols to serve the living and true God;* (1 Thessalonians 1:9)

Chapter 34

TAKE HEED

And Jesus answered and said unto them, **TAKE HEED** *that no man deceive you.* For many shall come in my name, saying, I am Christ; and *shall deceive many.* And ye shall hear of wars and rumours of wars: see that ye be not troubled: for all these things must come to pass, but the end is not yet. For nation shall rise against nation, and kingdom against kingdom: and there shall be famines, and pestilences, and earthquakes, in divers places. All these are the *beginning* of sorrows. (Matthew 24:4-8)

And as he sat upon the mount of Olives over against the temple, Peter and James and John and Andrew asked him privately, Tell us, when shall these things be? and what shall be the sign when all these things shall be fulfilled? And Jesus answering them began to say, **TAKE HEED** *lest any man deceive you:* For *many* shall come in my name, saying, I am Christ; and *shall deceive many.* And when ye shall hear of wars and rumours of wars, be ye not troubled: for such things must needs be; but the end shall not be yet. For nation shall rise against nation, and kingdom against kingdom: and there shall be earthquakes in divers places, and there shall be famines and troubles: these are the *beginnings* of sorrows. (Mark 13:3-8)

The light of the body is the eye: therefore when thine eye is single, thy whole body also is full of light; but when thine eye is evil, thy body also is full of darkness. **TAKE HEED** ***therefore that the light which is in thee be not darkness.*** If thy whole body therefore be full of light, having no part dark, the whole shall be full of light, as when the bright shining of a candle doth give thee light. (Luke 11:34-36)

And they asked him, saying, Master, but when shall these things be? and what sign will there be when these things shall come to pass? And he said, **TAKE HEED** ***that ye be not deceived:*** for *many shall come in my name, saying, I am Christ; and the time draweth near: go ye not therefore after them.* But when ye shall hear of wars and commotions, *be not terrified:* for these things must first come to pass; but the end is not by and by. (Luke 21:7-9)

Heaven and earth shall pass away: *but my words shall not pass away.* And **TAKE HEED** ***to yourselves,*** lest at any time your hearts be overcharged with surfeiting, and drunkenness, and cares of this life, and so that day come upon you unawares. *For as a <u>snare</u> shall it come on ALL them that dwell on the face of the whole earth. <u>Watch</u> ye therefore, and pray always, that ye may be accounted <u>worthy</u> to escape* all these things that shall come to pass, and to stand before the Son of man. (Luke 21:33-36)

And if some of the branches be broken off, and thou, being a wild olive tree, wert grafted in among them, and with them partakest of the root and fatness of the olive tree; Boast *not* against the branches. But if thou boast, thou bearest not the root, but the root thee. Thou wilt say then, The branches were broken off, that I might be grafted in. Well; because of unbelief they were broken off, and thou standest by faith. Be *not* highminded, but fear: For if God spared not the natural branches, **TAKE HEED *lest he also spare not thee. Behold therefore the goodness and severity of God:*** on them which fell, severity; but toward thee, goodness, *if* thou continue in his goodness: otherwise thou also shalt be cut off. And they also, *if* they abide *not* still in unbelief, shall be grafted in: for God is able to graft them in again. For *if* thou wert cut out of the olive tree which is wild by nature, and wert grafted contrary to nature into a good olive tree: how much more shall these, which be the natural branches, be grafted into their own olive tree? (Romans 11:17-24)

According to the grace of God which is given unto me, as a wise masterbuilder, I have laid the foundation, and another buildeth thereon. But ***let every man* TAKE HEED *how he buildeth thereupon.*** For other foundation can no man lay than that is laid, which is *Jesus Christ.* Now if any man build upon this foundation gold, silver, precious stones, wood, hay, stubble; *Every man's work shall be made manifest:* for the day shall declare it, because *it shall be revealed by fire; and the fire shall try every man's work of what sort it is.* If any man's work <u>abide</u> which he hath built thereupon, he shall receive a *reward.* If any man's work shall be <u>burned,</u> he shall *suffer loss*: but he himself shall be saved; yet so as by fire. (1 Corinthians 3:10-15)

Wherefore ***let him that thinketh he standeth* TAKE HEED *lest he fall*.** There hath no temptation taken you but such as is common to man: but *God is faithful, who will not suffer you to be tempted above that ye are able; but will with the temptation also make a way to escape, that ye may be able to bear it.* (1 Corinthians 10:12-13)

Meditate upon these things; give thyself <u>wholly</u> to them; that thy profiting may appear to all. **TAKE HEED** unto thyself, and unto the doctrine; continue in them: for ***in doing this thou shalt both save thyself, and them that hear thee.*** (1 Timothy 4:15-16)

Wherefore (as the Holy Ghost saith, *<u>To day</u> if ye will hear his voice, Harden not your hearts,* as in the provocation, in the day of temptation in the wilderness: When your fathers tempted me, proved me, and saw my works forty years. Wherefore I was grieved with that generation, and said, *They do alway err in their heart;* and they have not known my ways. So I sware in my wrath, They shall not enter into my rest.) **TAKE HEED, *brethren, lest there be in any of you an evil heart of unbelief, in departing from the living God.*** But exhort one another <u>daily</u>, while it is called To day; *lest any of you be hardened through the <u>deceitfulness</u> of sin.* For we are made partakers of Christ, if we hold the

beginning of our confidence stedfast unto the end;
(Hebrews 3:7-14)

Chapter 35

SAVED

And, behold, one came and said unto him, Good Master, what good thing shall I do, that I may have eternal life? And he said unto him, Why callest thou me good? there is none good but one, that is, God: but *if thou wilt enter into life, keep the commandments.* He saith unto him, Which? Jesus said, Thou shalt do no murder, Thou shalt not commit adultery, Thou shalt not steal, Thou shalt not bear false witness, Honour thy father and thy mother: and, Thou shalt love thy neighbour as thyself. The young man saith unto him, All these things have I kept from my youth up: what lack I yet? Jesus said unto him, *If thou wilt be perfect, go and sell that thou hast, and give to the poor, and thou shalt have treasure in heaven: and come and follow me.* But when the young man heard that saying, he went away sorrowful: for he had great possessions. Then said Jesus unto his disciples, Verily I say unto you, That a rich man shall hardly enter into the kingdom of heaven. And again I say unto you, It is easier for a camel to go through the eye of a needle, than for a rich man to enter into the kingdom of God. When his disciples heard it, they were exceedingly amazed, saying, Who then can be **SAVED**? But Jesus beheld them, and said unto them, *With men this is impossible; but with God all things are possible.* (Matthew 19:16-26)

And Jesus answered and said unto them, *Take heed that no man deceive you.* For many shall come in my name, saying, I am Christ; and *shall deceive many.* And ye shall hear of wars and rumours of wars: see that ye be not troubled: for all these things must come to pass, but the end is not yet. For nation shall rise against nation, and kingdom against kingdom: and there shall be famines, and pestilences, and earthquakes, in divers places. All these are the beginning of sorrows. Then shall they deliver you up to be afflicted, and shall kill you: and ye shall be hated of all nations for my name's sake. And then shall many be offended, and shall betray one another, and shall hate one another. And many false prophets shall rise, and *shall deceive many.* And <u>because iniquity shall abound, the love of many shall wax cold</u>. **But** ***he that shall endure unto the end, the same shall be*** **SAVED**. (Matthew 24:4-13)

And when he was gone forth into the way, there came one running, and kneeled to him, and asked him, Good Master, what shall I do that I may inherit eternal life? And Jesus said unto him, Why callest thou me good? there is none good but one, that is, God. *Thou knowest the commandments,* Do not commit adultery, Do not kill, Do not steal, Do not bear false witness, Defraud not, Honour thy father and mother. And he answered and said unto him, Master, all these have I observed from my youth. Then Jesus beholding him loved him, and said unto him, *One thing thou lackest: go thy way, sell* *whatsoever thou hast, and give to the poor, and thou shalt have <u>treasure</u> in heaven: and come, take up the cross, and follow me.* And he was sad at that saying, and went away grieved: for he had great possessions. And Jesus looked round about, and saith unto his disciples, How *hardly* shall they that have riches enter into the kingdom of God! And the disciples were astonished at his words. But Jesus answereth again, and saith unto them, Children, how *hard* is it for them that trust in riches to enter into the kingdom of God! It is easier for a camel to go through the eye of a needle, than for a rich man to enter into the kingdom of God. And they were astonished out of measure, saying among themselves, **Who then can be SAVED**? And Jesus looking upon them saith, *With men it is impossible, but not with God: for with God all things are possible.* (Mark 10:17-27)

And Jesus answering them began to say, *Take heed lest any man deceive you:* For many shall come in my name, saying, I am Christ; and *shall deceive many.* And when ye shall hear of wars and rumours of wars, be ye not troubled: for such things must needs be; but the end shall not be yet. For nation shall rise against nation, and kingdom against kingdom: and there shall be earthquakes in divers places, and there shall be famines and troubles: these are the *beginnings* of sorrows. But take heed to yourselves: for they shall deliver you up to councils; and in the synagogues ye shall be beaten: and ye shall be brought before rulers and kings for my sake, for a testimony against them. And *the gospel must first be published among all nations.*

But when they shall lead you, and deliver you up, take no thought beforehand what ye shall speak, neither do ye premeditate: but whatsoever shall be given you in that hour, that speak ye: for it is not ye that speak, but the Holy Ghost. Now the brother shall betray the brother to death, and the father the son; and children shall rise up against their parents, and shall cause them to be put to death. And ye shall be hated of all men for my name's sake: but *he that shall endure unto the end, the same shall be* **SAVED**. (Mark 13:5-13)

And he said unto them, Go ye into all the world, and preach the gospel to every creature. *He that believeth and is baptized shall be* **SAVED**; but he that believeth *not* shall be damned. (Mark 16:15-16)

Then said one unto him, Lord, are there few that be **SAVED**? And he said unto them, *Strive to enter in at the strait gate: for many, I say unto you, will seek to enter in, and shall not be able.* (Luke 13:23-24)

And a certain ruler asked him, saying, Good Master, what shall I do to inherit eternal life? And Jesus said unto him, Why callest thou me good? none is good, save one, that is, God. *Thou knowest the commandments,* Do not commit adultery, Do not kill, Do not steal, Do not bear false witness, Honour thy father and thy mother. And he said, All these have I kept from my youth up. Now when Jesus heard these things, he said unto him, *Yet lackest thou one thing: sell all that thou hast, and distribute unto the poor, and thou shalt have <u>treasure</u> in* *heaven: and come, follow me.* And when he heard this, he was very sorrowful: for he was very rich. And when Jesus saw that he was very sorrowful, he said, *How hardly shall they that have riches enter into the kingdom of God!* For it is easier for a camel to go through a needle's eye, than for a rich man to enter into the kingdom of God. And they that heard it said, **Who then can be SAVED**? And he said, *The things which are impossible with men are possible with God.* (Luke 18:18-27)

And as Moses lifted up the serpent in the wilderness, even so must the Son of man be lifted up: That whosoever believeth in him should not perish, but have eternal life. For God so loved the world, that he gave his only begotten Son, that whosoever believeth in him should not perish, but have everlasting life. **For God sent not his Son into the world to condemn the world; but that the world through him might be SAVED.** (John 3:14-17)

But I receive not testimony from man: but these things I say, *that ye might be* **SAVED**. (John 5:34)

I am the door: by me if any man enter in, he shall be SAVED, and shall go in and out, and find pasture. The *thief* cometh not, but for to steal, and to kill, and to destroy: *I am come that they might have life, and that they might have it more abundantly.* (John 10:9-10)

But this is that which was spoken by the prophet Joel; And it shall come to pass *in the last days, saith God, I will pour out of my Spirit upon all flesh:* and your sons and your daughters shall prophesy, and your young men shall see visions, and your old men shall dream dreams: And on my servants and on my handmaidens I will pour out in those days of my Spirit; and they shall prophesy: And I will shew wonders in heaven above, and signs in the earth beneath; blood, and fire, and vapour of smoke: The sun shall be turned into darkness, and the moon into blood, before the great and notable day of the Lord come: And it shall come to pass, that *whosoever shall call on the name of the Lord shall be* **SAVED**. (Acts 2:16-21)

Be it known unto you all, and to all the people of Israel, that by the name of Jesus Christ of Nazareth, whom ye crucified, whom God raised from the dead, even by him doth this man stand here before you whole. This is the stone which was set at nought of you builders, which is become the head of the corner. *Neither is there salvation in any other: for there is none other name under heaven given among men, whereby we must be* **SAVED**. (Acts 4:10-12)

And brought them out, and said, Sirs, what must I do to be **SAVED**? And they said, *Believe on the Lord Jesus Christ, and thou shalt be* **SAVED**, *and thy house.* (Acts 16:30-31)

For when we were yet without strength, in due time *Christ died for the ungodly.* For scarcely for a righteous man will one die: yet peradventure for a good man some would even dare to die. But God commendeth his love toward us, in that, *while we were yet sinners, Christ died for us.* Much more then, being now justified by his blood, ***we shall be SAVED from wrath through him.*** For if, when we were enemies, we were *reconciled to God* by the death of his Son, much more, being reconciled, we ***shall be SAVED by his life.*** (Romans 5:6-10)

For we are SAVED by hope: but hope that is seen is not hope: for what a man seeth, why doth he yet hope for? But if we hope for that we see not, then do we with patience wait for it. (Romans 8:24-25)

Brethren, ***my heart's desire and prayer to God for Israel is, that they might be SAVED.*** (Romans 10:1)

But what saith it? The word is nigh thee, even in thy mouth, and in thy heart: that is, the word of faith, which we preach; That ***if thou shalt confess with thy mouth the Lord Jesus, and shalt believe in thine heart that God hath raised him from the dead, thou shalt be SAVED.*** For with the *heart* man <u>believeth</u> unto righteousness; and with the *mouth* <u>confession</u> is made unto salvation. For the scripture saith, *Whosoever believeth on him shall not be ashamed.* For there is no difference between the Jew and the Greek: for the same Lord over all is rich unto all that call upon him. ***For whosoever shall call upon the name of the Lord shall be SAVED.*** (Romans 10:8-13)

For *the preaching of the cross* is to them that perish foolishness; but ***unto us which are SAVED it is the power of God.*** (1 Corinthians 1:18)

Give none offence, neither to the Jews, nor to the Gentiles, nor to the church of God: *Even as I please all men in all things*, not seeking mine own profit, but **the profit of many, that they may be SAVED**. (1 Corinthians 10:32-33)

Moreover, brethren, I declare unto you the ***gospel*** which I preached unto you, which also ye have received, and wherein ye stand; **By which also ye are SAVED**, if ye keep in memory what I preached unto you, unless ye have believed in vain. For I delivered unto you first of all that which I also received, how that *Christ died for our sins according to the scriptures; And that he was buried, and that he rose again the third day according to the scriptures:* And that he was seen of Cephas (Peter), then of the twelve: After that, he was seen of above five hundred brethren at once; of whom the greater part remain unto this present, but some are fallen asleep. After that, he was seen of James; then of all the apostles. And last of all he was seen of me (Paul) also, as of one born out of due time. (1 Corinthians 15:1-8)

Now thanks be unto God, which always causeth us to *triumph in Christ*, and maketh manifest the savour of his knowledge by us in every place. For **we are unto God a <u>sweet</u> savour of Christ, in them that are SAVED**, and in them that perish: To the one we are the <u>savour of death unto death</u>; and to the other the *savour of life unto life*. And who is sufficient for these things? (2 Corinthians 2:14-16)

And you hath he quickened, who were dead in trespasses and sins; Wherein in time past ye walked according to the course of this world, according to the prince of the power of the air, the spirit that now worketh in the children of disobedience: Among whom also we all had our conversation in times past in the lusts of our flesh, fulfilling the desires of the flesh and of the mind; and were by nature the children of wrath, even as others. **But God, who is rich in mercy, for his great love wherewith he loved us, Even when we were dead in sins, hath quickened us together with Christ, (by grace ye are SAVED;)** And hath raised us up together, and made us sit together in heavenly places in Christ Jesus: That in the ages to come he might shew the exceeding riches of his grace in his kindness toward us through Christ Jesus. ***For by grace are ye* SAVED *through faith;*** and that not of yourselves: it is the gift of God: Not of works, lest any man should boast. For we are his workmanship, *created in Christ Jesus unto good works,* which God hath before ordained that we should walk in them. (Ephesians 2:1-10)

I exhort therefore, that, first of all, supplications, prayers, intercessions, and giving of thanks, be made for *all* men; For <u>kings</u>, and for all that are in <u>authority</u>; that we may lead a quiet and peaceable life in all godliness and honesty. For this is good and acceptable in the sight of God our Saviour; ***Who will have all men to be* SAVED, *and to come unto the knowledge of the truth.*** For there is one God, and ***one*** mediator between God and men, the man *Christ Jesus;* Who gave himself a ransom for all, to be testified in due time. (1 Timothy 2:1-6)

For God hath not given us the spirit of fear; but of power, and of love, and of a sound mind. Be not thou therefore ashamed of the testimony of our Lord, nor of me his prisoner: but *be thou partaker of the afflictions of the gospel* according to the power of God; **Who hath SAVED us,** and called us with an holy calling, not according to our works, but according to his own purpose and grace, which was given us in Christ Jesus before the world began, But is now made manifest by the appearing of ***our Saviour Jesus Christ, who hath abolished death, and hath brought life and immortality to light through the gospel:*** (2 Timothy 1:7-10)

Put them in mind to be subject to principalities and powers, to obey magistrates, to be ready to every good work, To speak evil of no man, to be no brawlers, but gentle, shewing all meekness unto all men. For we ourselves also <u>were</u> sometimes foolish, disobedient, deceived, serving divers lusts and pleasures, living in malice and envy, hateful, and hating one another. But after that the kindness and love of God our Saviour toward man appeared, Not by works of righteousness which *we* have done, but *according to his mercy he* **SAVED us,** by the washing of regeneration, and renewing of the Holy Ghost; Which he shed on us abundantly through *Jesus Christ our Saviour;* That being justified by his grace, we should be made heirs according to the hope of eternal life. (Titus 3:1-7)

For it is better, *if the will of God be so, that ye suffer for well doing,* than for evil doing. For *Christ also hath once suffered for sins, <u>the just for the unjust</u>,* that he might bring us to God, being put to death in the flesh, but quickened by the Spirit: By which also he went and preached unto the spirits in prison; Which sometime were disobedient, when once the longsuffering of God waited in the days of Noah, while the ark was a preparing, wherein few, that is, eight souls were **SAVED** by water. The like figure whereunto even baptism doth also now **SAVE** us (not the putting away of the filth of the flesh, but the answer of a good conscience toward God,) by the resurrection of Jesus Christ: Who is gone into heaven, and is on the right hand of God; angels and authorities and powers being made subject unto him. (1 Peter 3:17-22)

Beloved, *think it not strange concerning the fiery trial which is to try you,* as though some strange thing happened unto you: But rejoice, inasmuch as *ye are partakers of Christ's sufferings;* that, when his glory shall be revealed, ye may be glad also with exceeding joy. *If ye be reproached for the name of Christ, happy are ye; for the spirit of glory and of God resteth upon you:* on their part he is evil spoken of, but on your part he is glorified. But let none of you suffer as a murderer, or as a thief, or as an evildoer, or as a busybody in other men's matters. Yet *if any man suffer as a Christian, let him not be ashamed;* but let him glorify God on this behalf. For the time is come that *judgment must begin at the house of God:* and if it first begin at us, what shall the end be of them that obey not the gospel of

God? And *if the righteous scarcely be* **SAVED**, where shall the ungodly and the sinner appear? Wherefore let them that suffer according to the will of God *commit the keeping of their souls to him in well doing,* as unto a faithful Creator. (1 Peter 4:12-19)

But there were false prophets also among the people, even as there shall be false teachers among you, who privily shall bring in damnable heresies, even denying the Lord that bought them, and bring upon themselves swift destruction. And many shall follow their pernicious ways; by reason of whom the way of truth shall be evil spoken of. And through covetousness shall they with feigned words make merchandise of you: whose judgment now of a long time lingereth not, and their damnation slumbereth not. For if God spared not the angels that sinned, but cast them down to hell, and delivered them into chains of darkness, to be reserved unto judgment; And spared not the old world, **but SAVED** *Noah the eighth person, a preacher of righteousness,* bringing in the flood upon the world of the ungodly; And turning the cities of Sodom and Gomorrha into ashes condemned them with an overthrow, *making them an ensample* unto those that after should live ungodly; And delivered just Lot, vexed with the filthy conversation of the wicked: (For that righteous man dwelling among them, in seeing and hearing, vexed his righteous soul from day to day with their unlawful deeds;) The Lord knoweth how to deliver the godly out of temptations, and to reserve the unjust unto the day of judgment to be punished: (2 Peter 2:1-9)

Beloved, when I gave all diligence to write unto you of the common salvation, it was needful for me to write unto you, and exhort you that *ye should earnestly contend for the faith which was once delivered unto the saints.* For there are certain men crept in unawares, who were before of old ordained to this condemnation, ungodly men, turning the grace of our God into lasciviousness, and denying the only Lord God, and our Lord Jesus Christ. I will therefore put you in remembrance, though ye once knew this, how that the Lord, having **SAVED the people out of the land of Egypt,** afterward destroyed them that believed not. And the angels which kept not their first estate, but left their own habitation, he hath reserved in everlasting chains under darkness unto the judgment of the great day. Even as Sodom and Gomorrha, and the cities about them in like manner, giving themselves over to fornication, and going after strange flesh, *are set forth for an example,* suffering the vengeance of eternal fire. (Jude 1:3-7)

And there came unto me one of the seven angels which had the seven vials full of the seven last plagues, and talked with me, saying, *Come hither, I will shew thee the bride, the Lamb's wife.* And he carried me away in the spirit to a great and high mountain, and shewed me **that great city, the holy Jerusalem, <u>descending out of heaven from God</u>**, Having the glory of God: and her *light* was like unto a stone most precious, even like a jasper stone, clear as crystal; And had a _wall_ great and high, and had _twelve gates_, and at the gates _twelve angels_, and names written thereon, which are the names of the _twelve tribes_ of the children of Israel: On the _east_ three gates; on the _north_ three gates; on the _south_ three gates; and on the _west_ three gates. And the wall of the city had _twelve foundations_, and in them the names of the _twelve apostles_ of the Lamb. And he that talked with me had a golden reed to _measure_ the city, and the gates thereof, and the wall thereof. And the city lieth foursquare, and the length is as large as the breadth: and he measured the city with the reed, twelve thousand furlongs. *The length and the breadth and the height of it are equal.* And he measured the wall thereof, an hundred and forty and four cubits, according to the measure of a man, that is, of the angel. And the building of the _wall_ of it was of jasper: and the _city_ was pure gold, like unto clear glass. And _the foundations_ of the wall of the city were garnished with all manner of precious stones. The _first_ foundation was jasper; the _second_, sapphire; the _third_, a chalcedony; the _fourth_, an emerald; The _fifth_, sardonyx; the _sixth_, sardius; the _seventh_, chrysolyte; the _eighth_, beryl; the _ninth_, a topaz; the _tenth_, a chrysoprasus; the _eleventh_, a jacinth; the _twelfth_, an amethyst. And the _twelve gates_ were twelve pearls: every several gate was of one pearl: and the _street_ of the city was pure gold, as it were transparent glass. And *I saw* **no** _temple_ therein: **for the Lord God Almighty and the Lamb are the temple of it.** And the city had no need of the sun, neither of the moon, to shine in it: for *the glory of God did lighten it, and the Lamb is the light thereof.* **And the nations of them which are**

SAVED *shall walk in the light of it:* and **the kings** *of the earth do bring their glory and honour into it.* And *the gates* of it shall *not be shut* at all by day: for there shall be *no night* there. And they shall bring the glory and honour of the nations into it. And **there shall in no wise enter** into it any thing that defileth, neither whatsoever worketh abomination, or maketh a lie: but *they which are written in the Lamb's book of life.* (Revelation 21:9-27)

Chapter 36

SALVATION

And his father Zacharias was filled with the Holy Ghost, and prophesied, saying, *Blessed be the Lord God of Israel; for he hath visited and redeemed his people,* **And hath raised up an horn of SALVATION *for us in the house of his servant David;* As he spake by the mouth of his holy prophets,** which have been since the world began: That we should be saved from our enemies, and from the hand of all that hate us; To perform the mercy promised to our fathers, and to remember his holy covenant; The oath which he sware to our father Abraham, That he would grant unto us, that we being delivered out of the hand of our enemies might serve him without fear, In holiness and righteousness before him, all the days of our life. And thou, child, shalt be called *the prophet* of the Highest: for thou shalt go before the face of the Lord *to prepare his ways;* **To give knowledge of SAVLATION *unto his people by the remission of their sins,*** Through the tender mercy of our God; whereby the dayspring from on high hath visited us, *To give light to them that sit in darkness and in the shadow of death, to guide our feet into the way of peace.* (Luke 1:67-79)

And, behold, there was a man in Jerusalem, whose name was *Simeon;* and the same man was *just and devout,* waiting for the consolation of Israel: and the Holy Ghost was upon him. And it was revealed unto him by the Holy Ghost, that he should not see death, before he had seen the Lord's Christ. And he came by the Spirit into the temple: and when the parents brought in the child Jesus, to do for him after the custom of the law, Then took he him up in his arms, and blessed God, and said, *Lord, now lettest thou thy servant depart in peace, according to thy word: For mine eyes have seen thy* **SALVATION**, ***Which thou hast prepared before the face of all people;*** A light to lighten the Gentiles, and the glory of thy people Israel. (Luke 2:25-32)

Now in the fifteenth year of the reign of Tiberius Caesar, Pontius Pilate being governor of Judaea, and Herod being tetrarch of Galilee, and his brother Philip tetrarch of Ituraea and of the region of Trachonitis, and Lysanias the tetrarch of Abilene, Annas and Caiaphas being the high priests, *the word of God came unto John the son of Zacharias in the wilderness.* And he came into all the country about *Jordan, preaching the baptism of repentance for the remission of sins;* As it is written in the book of the words of Esaias the prophet, saying, The voice of one crying in the wilderness, *Prepare ye the way of the Lord, make his paths straight. Every valley shall be filled, and every mountain and hill shall be brought low; and the crooked shall be made straight, and the rough ways shall be made smooth;* ***And all flesh shall see the*** **SALVATION** ***of God.*** (Luke 3:1-6)

And Jesus entered and passed through Jericho. And, behold, there was a man named *Zacchaeus,* which was the chief among the publicans, and he was rich. And he sought to see Jesus who he was; and could not for the press, because he was little of stature. And he ran before, and climbed up into a sycomore tree to see him: for he was to pass that way. And when Jesus came to the place, he looked up, and saw him, and said unto him, *Zacchaeus, make haste, and come down; for to day I must abide at thy house.* And he made haste, and came down, and received him joyfully. And when they saw it, they all murmured, saying, That he was gone to be guest with a man that is a sinner. And Zacchaeus stood, and said unto the Lord: **Behold, Lord, the half of my goods** *I give to the poor; and if I have taken any thing from any man by false accusation, I restore him fourfold.* And Jesus said unto him, **This day is SALVATION *come to this house,*** forsomuch as he also is a son of Abraham. *For the Son of man is come to seek and to save that which was lost.* (Luke 19:1-10)

Then Peter, filled with the Holy Ghost, said unto them, Ye rulers of the people, and elders of Israel, If we this day be examined of the good deed done to the impotent man, *by what means he is made whole;* Be it known unto you all, and to all the people of Israel, that *by the name of Jesus Christ of Nazareth, whom ye crucified, whom God raised from the dead, even by him doth this man stand here before you whole.* This is the stone which was set at nought of you builders, which is become the *head* of the corner. **Neither is there SALVATION *in any*** *other: for there is none other name under heaven given among men, whereby we must be saved.* (Acts 4:8-12)

Of this man's seed hath God according to his promise raised unto Israel a Saviour, Jesus: When <u>John</u> had first preached <u>before</u> his coming the baptism of repentance to all the people of Israel. And as John fulfilled his course, he said, Whom think ye that I am? I am not he. But, behold, there cometh one after me, whose shoes of his feet I am not worthy to loose. Men and brethren, children of the stock of Abraham, and **whosoever among you <u>feareth God</u>, to you is the word of this SALVATION sent.** (Acts 13:23-26)

For so hath the Lord commanded us (Paul and Barnabas), saying, I have set thee to be a light of the Gentiles, that thou shouldest be for **SALVATION *unto the ends of the earth.*** And when the Gentiles heard this, they were glad, and glorified the word of the Lord: and *as many as were ordained to eternal life believed.* (Acts 13:47-48)

For I am not ashamed of the ***gospel of Christ: for it is the power of God unto* SALVATION *to every one that believeth*;** to the Jew first, and also to the Greek. (Romans 1:16)

That if thou shalt confess with thy mouth the Lord Jesus, and shalt believe in thine heart that God hath raised him from the dead, thou shalt be saved. For with the *heart* man *believeth* unto righteousness; and with the *mouth* *confession* is made unto **SALVATION**. For the scripture saith, *Whosoever believeth on him shall not be ashamed.* For there is no difference between the Jew and the Greek: for the same Lord over all is rich unto all that call upon him. ***For whosoever shall call upon the name of the Lord shall be saved.*** (Romans 10:9-13)

Owe no man any thing, but to love one another: ***for*** *he that loveth another hath fulfilled the law.* For this, Thou shalt not commit adultery, Thou shalt not kill, Thou shalt not steal, Thou shalt not bear false witness, Thou shalt not covet; and if there be any other commandment, it is briefly comprehended in this saying, namely, *Thou shalt love thy neighbour as thyself.* Love worketh *no ill* to his neighbour: therefore *love is the fulfilling of the law.* And that, knowing the time, that *now it is high time to awake out of sleep:* for **now is our SALVATION** nearer than when we believed. The night is far spent, the day is at hand: let us therefore *cast off the works of darkness, and let us put on the armour of light.* Let us walk *honestly,* as in the day; not in rioting and drunkenness, not in chambering and wantonness, not in strife and envying. But *put ye on the Lord Jesus Christ,* and make *NOT* provision for the flesh, to fulfil the lusts thereof. (Romans 13:8-14)

We then, as workers together with him, beseech you also that ye receive not the grace of God in vain. (For he saith, I have heard thee in a time accepted, and in **the day of SALVATION** have I succoured thee: ***behold, now is the accepted time; behold, now is the day of* SALVATION**.) (2 Corinthians 6:1-2)

For though I made you sorry with a letter, I do not repent, though I did repent: for I perceive that *the same epistle hath made you sorry, though it were but for a season.* Now I rejoice, not that ye were made sorry, but that *ye sorrowed to repentance: for ye were made sorry after a godly manner,* that ye might receive damage by us in nothing. **For godly sorrow worketh repentance to SALVATION** not to be repented of: but the sorrow of the world worketh death. (2 Corinthians 7:8-10)

That we should be to the praise of his glory, *who first trusted in Christ.* In whom ye also trusted, after that **ye heard the word of truth, the gospel of your SALVATION**: in whom also after that ye believed, ye were *sealed with that holy Spirit* of promise, *Which is the earnest* of our inheritance until the redemption of the purchased possession, unto the praise of his glory. (Ephesians 1:12-14)

Finally, my brethren, be strong in the Lord, and in the power of his might. *Put on the whole armour of God, that ye may be able to stand against the wiles of the devil.* For we wrestle *not* against flesh and blood, but against principalities, against powers, against the rulers of the darkness of this world, against spiritual wickedness in high places. *Wherefore take unto you the whole armour of God, that ye may be able to withstand in the evil day, and having done all, to stand.* **Stand** therefore, having your loins girt about with truth, and having on the _breastplate_ of righteousness; And your _feet_ shod with the preparation of the gospel of peace; Above all, taking the _shield of faith_, wherewith ye shall be able to quench all the fiery darts of the wicked. And **take the helmet of SALVATION**, and the _sword of the Spirit, which is the word of God:_ Praying _always_ with _all_ prayer and supplication in the Spirit, and watching thereunto with _all_ perseverance and supplication for _all_ saints; (Ephesians 6:10-18)

Only let your conversation be as it becometh the gospel of Christ: that whether I come and see you, or else be absent, I may hear of your affairs, that ye _stand fast in one spirit, with one mind striving together for the faith of the gospel;_ And in nothing terrified by your adversaries: which is to them an evident token of perdition, but **to you of SALVATION, and that of God**. _For unto you it is given in the behalf of Christ, not only to believe on him, but also to suffer for his sake;_ (Phillipians 1:27-29)

Let this mind be in you, which was also in Christ Jesus: Who, being in the form of God, thought it not robbery to be equal with God: But _made himself of no reputation, and took upon him the form of a servant,_ and was made in the likeness of men: And being found in fashion as a man, he _humbled himself, and became obedient unto death, even the death of the cross._ **Wherefore God also hath highly exalted him, and given him a name which is above every name:** _That at the name of Jesus every knee should bow, of things in heaven,_ and things in earth, and things under the earth; And *that every tongue should confess that Jesus Christ is Lord, to the glory of God the Father.* Wherefore, my beloved, as ye have always obeyed, not as in my presence only, but now much more in my absence, **work out your own SALVATION with fear and trembling.** For it is God which worketh in you both to will and to do of his good pleasure. (Phillipians 2:5-13)

But ye, brethren, are not in darkness, that that day should overtake you as a thief. Ye are all the children of light, and the children of the day: we are not of the night, nor of darkness. Therefore *let us not sleep, as do others; but let us watch and be sober.* For they that sleep sleep in the night; and they that be drunken are drunken in the night. But **let us, who are of the day, be sober, putting on the breastplate of faith and love; and for an helmet, the hope of SALVATION.** For God hath not appointed us to wrath, but **to obtain SALVATION by our Lord Jesus Christ,** Who died for us, that, whether we wake or sleep, we should live together with him. (1 Thessalonians 5:4-10)

For the grace of God that bringeth SALVATION hath appeared to all men, *Teaching us that, denying ungodliness and worldly lusts, we should live soberly, righteously, and godly, in this present world;* Looking for that blessed hope, and the glorious appearing of the great God and our Saviour Jesus Christ; Who gave himself for us, that he might redeem us from all iniquity, and purify unto himself a peculiar people, *zealous of good works.* (Titus 2:11-14)

But to which of the *angels* said he at any time, Sit on my right hand, until I make thine enemies thy footstool? Are they not **all ministering spirits, sent forth to minister for them who shall be heirs of SALVATION**? (Hebrews 1:13-14)

For if the word spoken by angels was stedfast, and *every transgression and disobedience received a just recompence of reward;* **How shall we escape, if we neglect so great SALVATION**; which at the first began to be spoken by the Lord, and was confirmed unto us by them that heard him; God also bearing them witness, both with signs and wonders, and with divers miracles, and gifts of the Holy Ghost, according to his own will? (Hebrews 2:2-4)

But we see *Jesus,* who was made a little lower than the angels for the suffering of death, crowned with glory and honour; that *he by the grace of God should taste death for every man.* For it became him, for whom are all things, and by whom are all things, **in bringing many sons unto glory, to make the captain of their SALVATION perfect through sufferings.** (Hebrews 2:9-10)

So also *Christ glorified* **not** *himself to be made an high priest;* but he that said unto him, Thou art my Son, to day have I begotten thee. As he saith also in another place, Thou art a priest for ever after the order of Melchisedec. Who in the days of his flesh, when he had offered up prayers and supplications with strong crying and tears unto him that was able to save him from death, and was heard in that he feared; *Though he were a Son, yet learned he obedience by the things which he suffered;* **And being made perfect, he became the author of eternal SALVATION unto all them that <u>obey</u> him;** (Hebrews 5:5-9)

For it is *impossible* for those who were once enlightened, and have tasted of the heavenly gift, and were made partakers of the Holy Ghost, And have tasted the good word of God, and the powers of the world to come, *If they shall fall away,* to renew them again unto repentance; *seeing they crucify to themselves the Son of God afresh, and put him to an open shame.* For the earth which drinketh in the rain that cometh oft upon it, and bringeth forth herbs meet for them by whom it is dressed, receiveth blessing from God: But that which beareth thorns and briers is rejected, and is nigh unto cursing; whose end is to be burned. **<u>But, beloved, we are persuaded better things of you, and things that accompany</u> SALVATION**, though we thus speak. For God is not unrighteous to forget your work and labour of love, which ye have shewed toward his name, in that *ye have ministered to the saints, and do minister.* And we desire that every one of you do *shew the same diligence to the full assurance of hope unto the end:* That ye be not slothful, but followers of them who through faith and patience inherit the promises. (Hebrews 6:4-12)

For *Christ* is not entered into the holy places made with hands, which are the *figures* of the true; but *into heaven itself, now to appear in the presence of God for us:* Nor yet that he should offer himself often, as the high priest entereth into the holy place every year with blood of others; For then must he often have suffered since the foundation of the world: but *now once in the end of the world hath he appeared to put away sin by the sacrifice of himself.* And as it is appointed unto men once to die, but after this the judgment: **So Christ was once offered to bear the sins of many; and unto them that look for him shall he appear the second time without sin unto SALVATION.** (Hebrews 9:24-28)

Blessed be the God and Father of our Lord Jesus Christ, which according to his abundant mercy hath begotten us again unto *a lively hope by the resurrection of Jesus Christ from the dead,* To an inheritance incorruptible, and undefiled, and that fadeth not away, reserved in heaven for you, **Who are kept by the power of God through faith unto SALVATION** ready to be revealed in the last time. Wherein ye greatly rejoice, though now for a season, if need be, ye are in heaviness through manifold temptations: That *the trial of your faith, being much more precious than of gold that perisheth, though it be tried with fire, might be found unto praise and honour and glory at the appearing of Jesus Christ:* Whom having not seen, ye love; in whom, though now ye see him not, yet believing, ye rejoice with joy unspeakable and full of glory: **Receiving the end of your faith, even the SALVATION *of your souls.*** Of which

SALVATION the prophets have enquired and searched diligently, who prophesied of the grace that should come unto you: (1 Peter 1:3-10)

Nevertheless we, according to his promise, look for new heavens and a new earth, wherein dwelleth righteousness. Wherefore, beloved, seeing that ye look for such things, *be diligent that ye may be found of him in peace, without spot, and blameless.* And account that **the longsuffering of our Lord is SALVATION**; even as our beloved brother Paul also according to the wisdom given unto him hath written unto you; (2 Peter 3:13-15)

Beloved, when I gave all diligence to write unto you of the common **SALVATION**, it was needful for me to write unto you, and exhort you that *ye should earnestly contend for the faith* which was once delivered unto the saints. For there are certain men crept in unawares, who were before of old ordained to this condemnation, ungodly men, turning the grace of our God into lasciviousness, and denying the only Lord God, and our Lord Jesus Christ. I will therefore put you in remembrance, though ye once knew this, how that the Lord, having saved the people out of the land of Egypt, afterward destroyed them that believed not. And the angels which kept not their first estate, but left their own habitation, he hath reserved in everlasting chains under darkness unto the judgment of the great day. Even as Sodom and Gomorrha, and the cities about them in like manner, giving themselves over to fornication, and going after strange flesh, are *set forth for an* *example,* suffering the vengeance of eternal fire. (Jude 1:3-7)

Chapter 37

EVERLASTING LIFE

And *every one that hath forsaken houses, or brethren, or sisters, or father, or mother, or wife, or children, or lands, for my name's sake, shall receive an hundredfold, and shall inherit* **EVERLASTING LIFE**. *But many that are first shall be last; and the last shall be first.* (Matthew 19:29-30)

And he said unto them, Verily I say unto you, There is ***no man that hath left house, or parents, or brethren, or wife, or children, for the kingdom of God's sake,*** *Who shall not receive manifold more in this present time, and in the world to come* **LIFE EVERLASTING.** (Luke 18:29-30)

And as Moses lifted up the serpent in the wilderness, even so must the Son of man be lifted up: ***That whosoever believeth in him should not perish, but have* ETERNAL LIFE.** *For God so loved the world, that he gave his only begotten Son, that whosoever believeth in him should not perish, but have* **EVERLASTING LIFE.** *For God sent not his Son into the world to condemn the world; but that the world through him might be saved.* He that believeth on him is not condemned: but he that believeth not is condemned already, because he hath not believed in the name of the only begotten Son of God. And this is the condemnation, that light is come into the world, and men loved darkness rather than light, because their deeds were evil. For every one that doeth evil hateth the light, neither cometh to the light, lest his deeds should be reproved. (John 3:14-20)

The Father loveth the Son, and hath given all things into his hand. ***He that believeth on the Son hath EVERLASTING LIFE***: and he that believeth not the Son shall not see life; but the wrath of God abideth on him. (John 3:35-36)

Now Jacob's well was there. Jesus therefore, being wearied with his journey, sat thus on the well: and it was about the sixth hour. There cometh a woman of Samaria to draw water: Jesus saith unto her, Give me to drink. (For his disciples were gone away unto the city to buy meat.) Then saith the woman of Samaria unto him, How is it that thou, being a Jew, askest drink of me, which am a woman of Samaria? for the Jews have no dealings with the Samaritans. Jesus answered and said unto her, If thou knewest the gift of God, and who it is that saith to thee, Give me to drink; thou wouldest have asked of him, and he would have given thee living water. The woman saith unto him, Sir, thou hast nothing to draw with, and the well is deep: from whence then hast thou that living water? Art thou greater than our father Jacob, which gave us the well, and drank thereof himself, and his children, and his cattle? Jesus answered and said unto her, Whosoever drinketh of this water shall thirst again: But whosoever drinketh of the water that I shall give him shall never thirst; but *the water that I shall give him shall be in him a well of water springing up into* **EVERLASTING LIFE**. (John 4:6-14)

That all men should honour the Son, even as they honour the Father. He that honoureth not the Son honoureth not the Father which hath sent him. **Verily, verily, I say unto you, He that heareth my word, and believeth on him that sent me, hath EVERLASTING LIFE**, *and shall not come into condemnation; but is passed from death unto life.* (John 5:23-24)

Jesus answered them and said, Verily, verily, I say unto you, Ye seek me, not because ye saw the miracles, but because ye did eat of the loaves, and were filled. *Labour not for the meat which perisheth, but for that meat which endureth unto* **EVERLASTING LIFE**, which the Son of man shall give unto you: for him hath God the Father sealed. Then said they unto him, What shall we do, that we might work the works of God? Jesus answered and said unto them, *This is the work of God, that ye believe on him whom he hath sent.* (John 6:26-29)

For I came down from heaven, not to do mine own will, but the will of him that sent me. And this is the Father's will which hath sent me, that of all which he hath given me I should lose nothing, but should raise it up again at the last day. And this is the will of him that sent me, *that every one which seeth the Son, and believeth on him, may have* **EVERLASTING LIFE**: *and I will raise him up at the last day.* (John 6:38-40)

No man can come to me, except the Father which hath sent me draw him: and I will raise him up at the last day. It is written in the prophets, *And they shall be all taught of God.* Every man therefore that hath _heard_, and hath _learned_ of the Father, cometh unto me. Not that any man hath seen the Father, save he which is of God, he hath seen the Father. Verily, verily, I say unto you, **He that believeth on me hath EVERLASTING LIFE.** (John 6:44-47)

Jesus cried and said, He that believeth on me, believeth not on me, but on him that sent me. And he that seeth me seeth him that sent me. *I am come a light into the world, that whosoever believeth on me should not abide in darkness.* And if any man hear my words, and believe not, I judge him not: for I came not to judge the world, but to save the world. He that rejecteth me, and receiveth not my words, hath one that judgeth him: the word that I have spoken, the same shall judge him in the last day. For I have not spoken of myself; but the Father which sent me, he gave me a commandment, what I should say, and what I should speak. And ***I know that his commandment is* LIFE EVERLASTING *whatsoever I speak therefore, even as the Father said unto me, so I speak.*** (John 12:44-50)

Know ye not, that to whom ye yield yourselves servants to obey, his servants ye are to whom ye obey; whether of sin unto death, or of obedience unto righteousness? But God be thanked, that ye were the servants of sin, but ye have obeyed from the heart that form of doctrine which was delivered you. Being then made free from sin, *ye became the servants of righteousness*. I speak after the manner of men because of the *infirmity* of your flesh: for as ye have yielded your members servants to uncleanness and to iniquity unto iniquity; even so now yield your members *servants to righteousness unto holiness*. For when ye were the *servants of sin,* ye were free from righteousness. What fruit had ye then in those things whereof ye are *now ashamed?* for the end of those things is death. **But now being made free from sin, and become servants to God, ye have your fruit unto holiness, and the end EVERLASTING LIFE.** For *the wages of sin is death;* but **the gift of God is ETERNAL LIFE through Jesus Christ our Lord.** (Romans 6:16-23)

Be not deceived; God is not mocked: for whatsoever a man soweth, that shall he also reap. For he that soweth to his flesh shall of the flesh reap corruption; but **he that soweth to the Spirit shall of the Spirit reap LIFE EVERLASTING.** And *let us not be weary in well doing:* for in due season we shall reap, *if* we faint not. As we have therefore opportunity, let us do good unto *all* men, *especially* unto them who are of the household of faith. (Galatians 6:7-10)

Chapter 38

ETERNAL LIFE

And, behold, one came and said unto him, ***Good Master, what good thing shall I do, that I may have* ETERNAL LIFE**? And he said unto him, Why callest thou me good? there is none good but one, that is, God: ***but** if thou wilt enter into life,* <u>***keep the commandments.***</u> He saith unto him, Which? Jesus said, Thou shalt do no murder, Thou shalt not commit adultery, Thou shalt not steal, Thou shalt not bear false witness, Honour thy father and thy mother: and, Thou shalt love thy neighbour as thyself. The young man saith unto him, All these things have I kept from my youth up: what lack I yet? Jesus said unto him, *If thou wilt be **perfect**, go and sell that thou hast, and give to the poor, and thou shalt have treasure in heaven: and come and follow me.* (Matthew 19:16-21)

When the Son of man shall come in his glory, and all the holy angels with him, then shall he sit upon the throne of his glory: And before him shall be gathered all nations: and he shall separate them one from another, as a shepherd divideth his sheep from the goats: And he shall set *the sheep on his right hand,* <u>but the goats on the left</u>. Then shall the King say unto them *on his right hand, Come, ye blessed of my Father, inherit the kingdom prepared for you from the foundation of the world:* For I was an <u>hungred</u>, and ye gave me meat: I was <u>thirsty</u>, and ye gave me drink: I was a <u>stranger</u>, and ye took me in: <u>Naked</u>, and ye clothed me: I was <u>sick</u>, and ye visited me: I was in <u>prison</u>, and ye came unto me. Then shall the righteous answer him, saying, Lord, when saw we thee an hungred, and fed thee? or thirsty, and gave thee drink? When saw we thee a stranger, and took thee in? or naked, and clothed thee? Or when saw we thee sick, or in prison, and came unto thee? And the King shall answer and say unto them, Verily I say unto you, *Inasmuch as ye have done it unto one of the least of these my brethren, ye have done it unto me.* Then shall he say also unto them on the left hand, Depart from me, ye cursed, into everlasting fire, prepared for the devil and his angels: For I was an hungred, and ye gave me no meat: I was thirsty, and ye gave me no drink: I was a stranger, and ye took me not in: naked, and ye clothed me not: sick, and in prison, and ye visited me not. Then shall they also answer him, saying, Lord, when saw we thee an hungred, or athirst, or a stranger, or naked, or sick, or in prison, and did not minister unto thee? Then shall he answer them, saying, Verily I say unto you, Inasmuch as ye did it *not* to one of the least of these, ye did it *not* to me. And these shall go away into everlasting punishment: ***but the <u>righteous</u> into* LIFE ETERNAL**. (Matthew 25:31-46)

And when he was gone forth into the way, there came one running, and kneeled to him, and asked him, ***Good Master, what shall I <u>do</u> that I may inherit* ETERNAL LIFE**? And Jesus said unto him, Why callest thou me good? there is none good but one, that is, God. **Thou knowest the commandments**, Do not commit adultery, Do not kill, Do not steal, Do not bear false witness, Defraud not, Honour thy father and mother. And he answered and said unto him, Master, all these have I observed from my youth. Then Jesus beholding him loved him, and said unto him, *One thing thou lackest: go thy way, sell whatsoever thou hast, and give to the poor, and thou shalt have treasure in heaven: and come, take up the cross, and follow me.* And he was sad at that saying, and went away grieved: for he had great possessions. And Jesus looked round about, and saith unto his disciples, How *hardly* shall they that have riches enter into the kingdom of God! And the disciples were astonished at his words. But Jesus answereth again, and saith unto them, Children, how *hard* is it for them that trust in riches to enter into the kingdom of God! It is easier for a camel to go through the eye of a needle, than for a rich man to enter into the kingdom of God. And they were astonished out of measure, saying among themselves, Who then can be saved? And Jesus looking upon them saith, *With men it is impossible, but not with God: for with God all things are possible.* (Mark 10:17-27)

Then Peter began to say unto him, Lo, we have left all, and have followed thee. And Jesus answered and said, Verily I say unto you, There is no man that hath *left* house, or brethren, or sisters, or father, or mother, or wife, or children, or lands, for my sake, and the gospel's, But he shall receive an hundredfold *now in this time*, houses, and brethren, and sisters, and mothers, and children, and lands, with persecutions; **and in the world to come ETERNAL LIFE.** ***But*** *many that are first shall be last; and the last first.* (Mark 10:28-31)

And, behold, a certain lawyer stood up, and tempted him, saying, Master, **what shall I <u>do</u> to inherit ETERNAL LIFE**? He said unto him, What is written in the law? how readest thou? And he answering said, *Thou shalt love the Lord thy God with all thy heart, and with all thy soul, and with all thy strength, and with all thy mind; and thy neighbour as thyself.* And he said unto him, **Thou hast answered right: this <u>do</u>, and thou shalt live.** But he, willing to justify himself, said unto Jesus, And who is my neighbour? And Jesus answering said, A certain man went down from Jerusalem to Jericho, and fell among thieves, which stripped him of his raiment, and wounded him, and departed, leaving him half dead. And by chance there came down a certain priest that way: and when he saw him, he passed by on the other side. And likewise a Levite, when he was at the place, came and looked on him, and passed by on the other side. But a certain Samaritan, as he journeyed, came where he was: and when he saw him, he had compassion on him, And went to him, and bound up his wounds, pouring in oil and wine, and set him on his own beast, and brought him to an inn, and took care of him. And on the morrow when he departed, he took out two pence, and gave them to the host, and said unto him, Take care of him; and whatsoever thou spendest more, when I come again, I will repay thee. Which now of these three, thinkest thou, was neighbour unto him that fell among the thieves? And he said, *He that shewed mercy on him.* Then said Jesus unto him, **Go, and do thou likewise.** (Luke 10:25-37)

And a certain ruler asked him, saying, *Good Master, what shall I do to inherit* **ETERNAL LIFE?** And Jesus said unto him, Why callest thou me good? none is good, save one, that is, God. *Thou knowest the commandments,* Do not commit adultery, Do not kill, Do not steal, Do not bear false witness, Honour thy father and thy mother. And he said, All these have I kept from my youth up. Now when Jesus heard these things, he said unto him, *Yet lackest thou one thing: sell all that thou hast, and distribute unto the poor, and thou shalt have treasure in heaven: and come, follow me.* And when he heard this, he was very sorrowful: for he was very rich. And when Jesus saw that he was very sorrowful, he said, How hardly shall they that have riches enter into the kingdom of God! For it is easier for a camel to go through a needle's eye, than for a rich man to enter into the kingdom of God. And they that heard it said, Who then can be saved? And he said, *The things which are impossible with men are possible with God.* Then Peter said, Lo, we have left all, and followed thee. And he said unto them, Verily I say unto you, *There is no man that hath left house, or parents, or brethren, or wife, or children, for the kingdom of God's sake, Who shall not receive manifold more in this present time, **and** in the world to come* **LIFE EVERLASTING.** (Luke 18:18-30)

And as Moses lifted up the serpent in the wilderness, even so must the Son of man be lifted up: *That whosoever believeth in him should not perish, but have* **ETERNAL LIFE.** *For God so loved the world, that he gave his only begotten Son,* *that whosoever believeth in him should not perish, but have* **EVERLASTING LIFE.** *For God sent not his Son into the world to condemn the world; but that the world through him might be saved.* He that believeth on him is not condemned: but he that believeth not is condemned already, because he hath not believed in the name of the only begotten Son of God. And this is the condemnation, that light is come into the world, and men loved darkness rather than light, because their deeds were evil. For every one that doeth evil hateth the light, neither cometh to the light, lest his deeds should be reproved. *But he that <u>**doeth**</u> truth cometh to the light, that his deeds may be made manifest, that they are wrought in God.* (John 3:14-21)

Say not ye, There are yet four months, and then cometh harvest? behold, I say unto you, *Lift up your eyes, and look on the fields; for they are white already to harvest.* And **he that reapeth receiveth wages, and gathereth fruit unto LIFE ETERNAL: that both he that soweth and he that reapeth may rejoice together.** And herein is that saying true, One soweth, and another reapeth. I sent you to reap that whereon ye bestowed no labour: other men laboured, and ye are entered into their labours. (John 4:35-38)

<u>**Search the scriptures**</u>**; for in them ye think ye have ETERNAL LIFE**: and they are they which testify of me (Jesus). (John 5:39)

Then Jesus said unto them, Verily, verily, I say unto you, Except ye eat the flesh of the Son of man, and drink his blood, ye have no life in you. *Whoso eateth my flesh, and drinketh my blood, hath* **ETERNAL LIFE**; and I will raise him up at the last day. For my flesh is meat indeed, and my blood is drink indeed. He that eateth my flesh, and drinketh my blood, dwelleth in me, and I in him. As the living Father hath sent me, and I live by the Father: so he that eateth me, even he shall live by me. This is that bread which came down from heaven: not as your fathers did eat manna, and are dead: *he that eateth of this bread shall live for ever.* (John 6:53-58)

Then Simon Peter answered him, Lord, to whom shall we go? *thou hast the words of* **ETERNAL LIFE**. And we believe and are sure that thou art that Christ, the Son of the living God. (John 6:68-69)

My sheep hear my voice, and I know them, and they follow me: And I give unto them **ETERNAL LIFE**; and they shall never perish, neither shall any man pluck them out of my hand. My Father, which gave them me, is greater than all; and no man is able to pluck them out of my Father's hand. I and my Father are one. (John 10:27-30)

And Jesus answered them, saying, The hour is come, that the Son of man should be glorified. Verily, verily, I say unto you, Except a corn of wheat fall into the ground and die, it abideth alone: *but if it die, it bringeth forth much fruit. He that loveth his life shall lose it; and he that hateth his life in this world shall keep it unto* **LIFE**

ETERNAL LIFE / 267

ETERNAL. If any man serve me, let him follow me; and where I am, there shall also my servant be: if any man serve me, him will my Father honour. (John 12:23-26)

These words spake Jesus, and lifted up his eyes to heaven, and said, Father, the hour is come; glorify thy Son, that thy Son also may glorify thee: *As thou hast given him power over all flesh, that he should give* **ETERNAL LIFE** *to as many as thou hast given him. And this is* **LIFE ETERNAL**, *that they might know thee the <u>only</u> true God, and Jesus Christ, whom thou hast sent.* I have glorified thee on the earth: I have finished the work which thou gavest me to do. And now, O Father, glorify thou me with thine own self with the glory which I had with thee before the world was. I have manifested thy name unto the men which thou gavest me out of the world: thine they were, and thou gavest them me; and *they have kept thy word.* (John 17:1-6)

For so hath the Lord commanded us (Paul and Barnabas), saying, I have set thee to be a light of the Gentiles, that thou shouldest be for *salvation unto the ends of the earth.* And when the Gentiles heard this, they were glad, and glorified the word of the Lord: and *as many as were ordained to* **ETERNAL LIVE** *believed.* (Acts 13:47-48)

Therefore thou art inexcusable, O man, whosoever thou art that judgest: for wherein thou judgest another, thou condemnest thyself; for thou that judgest doest the same things. But we are sure that the judgment of God is according to truth against them which commit such things. And thinkest thou this, O man, that judgest them which do such things, and doest the same, that thou shalt escape the judgment of God? *Or <u>despisest</u> thou the riches of his goodness and forbearance and longsuffering; not knowing that the goodness of God leadeth thee to repentance?* But after thy hardness and impenitent heart treasurest up unto thyself wrath against the day of wrath and revelation of the righteous judgment of God; *Who will render to every man according to his deeds:* **To them who by patient continuance in well doing seek for glory and honour and immortality, ETERNAL LIFE:** But unto them that are contentious, and do not obey the truth, but obey unrighteousness, indignation and wrath, Tribulation and anguish, upon every soul of man that doeth evil, of the Jew first, and also of the Gentile; *But glory, honour, and peace, to every man that worketh good,* to the Jew first, and also to the Gentile: For there is no respect of persons with God. (Romans 2:1-11)

That as sin hath reigned unto death, even so might ***grace reign through righteousness unto* ETERNAL LIFE** by Jesus Christ our Lord. (Romans 5:21)

Likewise reckon ye also yourselves to be dead indeed unto sin, but alive unto God through Jesus Christ our Lord. Let not sin therefore reign in your mortal body, that ye should obey it in the lusts thereof. Neither yield ye your members as instruments of unrighteousness unto sin: but yield yourselves unto God, as those that are alive from the dead, and your members as instruments of righteousness unto God. *For sin shall not have dominion over you:* for ye are not under the law, but under grace. What then? shall we sin, because we are not under the law, but under grace? God forbid. Know ye not, that to whom ye yield yourselves servants to obey, his servants ye are to whom ye obey; whether of sin unto death, or of obedience unto righteousness? But God be thanked, that ye were the servants of sin, but ye have obeyed from the heart that form of doctrine which was delivered you. *Being then made free from sin, ye became the servants of righteousness.* I speak after the manner of men because of the <u>infirmity</u> of your flesh: for as ye have yielded your members servants to uncleanness and to iniquity unto iniquity; even so *now yield your members servants to righteousness unto holiness.* For when ye were the servants of sin, ye were free from righteousness. What fruit had ye then in those things whereof ye are now ashamed? for the end of those things is death. **But now being made free from sin, and become servants to God, ye have your fruit unto holiness, and the end EVERLASTING LIFE**. For the wages of sin is death; but **the gift of God is ETERNAL LIFE through Jesus Christ our Lord.** (Romans 6:11-23)

But *they that will be rich* fall into temptation and a snare, and into many foolish and hurtful lusts, which drown men in destruction and perdition. *For the love of money is the root of all evil:* which while some coveted after, they have erred from the faith, and pierced themselves through with many sorrows. But thou, O man of God, *flee these things;* and follow after righteousness, godliness, faith, love, patience, meekness. ***Fight the good fight of faith, lay hold on* ETERNAL LIFE**, whereunto thou art also called, and hast professed a good profession before many witnesses. (1 Timothy 6:9-12)

Charge them that are rich in this world, that they be not highminded, nor trust in uncertain riches, but in the living God, who giveth us richly all things to enjoy; *That they do good,* that they *be rich in good works*, ready to distribute, willing to communicate; ***Laying up in store for themselves a good foundation against the time to come, that they may lay hold on* ETERNAL LIFE.** (1 Timothy 6:17-19)

Put them in mind to be subject to principalities and powers, to obey magistrates, *to be ready to every good work,* To speak evil of no man, to be no brawlers, but gentle, shewing all meekness unto all men. For we ourselves also were sometimes foolish, disobedient, deceived, serving divers lusts and pleasures, living in malice and envy, hateful, and hating one another. But after that the kindness and love of God our Saviour toward man appeared, Not by works of righteousness which we have done, but *according to his mercy he saved us,* by the washing of regeneration, and renewing of the Holy Ghost; Which he shed on us abundantly through Jesus Christ our Saviour; That being justified by his grace, ***we should be made heirs according to the hope of* ETERNAL LIFE.** This is a faithful saying, and these things I will that thou affirm constantly, that *they which have believed in God might be careful to maintain good works.* These things are good and profitable unto men. (Titus 3:1-8)

That which was from the beginning, which we have heard, which we have seen with our eyes, which we have looked upon, and our hands have handled, of the Word of life; (For the life was manifested, and we have seen it, and bear witness, and shew unto you that **ETERNAL LIFE**, *which was with the Father, and was manifested unto us;)* That which we have seen and heard declare we unto you, that ye also may have fellowship with us: and *truly our fellowship is with the Father, and with his Son Jesus Christ.* And these things write we unto you, that your joy may be full. This then is the message which we have heard of him, and declare unto you, that God is light, and in him is no darkness at all. If we say that we have fellowship with him, and walk in darkness, we lie, and do not the truth: *But if we walk in the light, as he is in the light, we have fellowship one with another, and the blood of Jesus Christ his Son cleanseth us from all sin.* If we say that we have no sin, we deceive ourselves, and the truth is not in us. If we confess our sins, he is faithful and just to forgive us our sins, and to cleanse us from all unrighteousness. If we say that we have not sinned, we make him a liar, and his word is not in us. (1 John 1:1-10)

Who is a liar but he that denieth that Jesus is the Christ? He is antichrist, that denieth the Father and the Son. Whosoever denieth the Son, the same hath not the Father: he that acknowledgeth the Son hath the Father also. Let that therefore abide in you, which ye have heard from the beginning. *If that which ye have heard from the beginning shall remain in you, ye also shall continue in the Son, and in the Father. And this is the promise that he hath promised us, even* **ETERNAL LIFE**. (1 John 2:22-25)

Marvel not, my brethren, if the world hate you. We know that we have passed from death unto life, because we love the brethren. He that loveth not his brother abideth in death. <u>Whosoever hateth his brother is a murderer</u>: and *ye know that no murderer hath* **ETERNAL LIFE** *abiding in him.* Hereby perceive we the love of God, because he laid down his life for us: and *we ought to lay down our lives for the brethren.* But whoso hath this world's good, and seeth his brother have need, and shutteth up his bowels of compassion from him, how dwelleth the love of God in him? My little children, *let us not love in word, neither in tongue; but in deed and in truth.* And hereby we know that we are of the truth, and shall assure our hearts before him. For if our heart condemn us, God is greater than our heart, and knoweth all things. Beloved, if our heart condemn us not, then have we confidence toward God. *And whatsoever we ask, we receive of him, because we keep his commandments, and do those things that are pleasing in his sight. And this is his commandment, That we should believe on the name of his Son Jesus Christ,* **and** *love one another, as he gave us commandment.* And he that keepeth his commandments dwelleth in him, and he in him. And hereby we know that he abideth in us, by the Spirit which he hath given us. (1 John 3:13-24)

And this is the record, ***that God hath given to us ETERNAL LIFE, and this life is in his Son.*** He that hath the Son hath life; and he that hath not the Son of God hath not life. These things have I written unto you that believe on the name of the Son of God; *that ye may **know** that ye have* **ETERNAL LIFE,** and *that ye may believe on the name of the Son of God.* (1 John 5:11-13)

All unrighteousness is sin: and there is a sin not unto death. *We know that whosoever is born of God sinneth not; **but** he that is begotten of God keepeth himself,* and that wicked one toucheth him not. And we know that we are of God, and the whole world lieth in wickedness. And we know that the Son of God is come, and hath given us an understanding, that we may know him that is true, and ***we are in him that is true, even in his Son Jesus Christ. This is the true God, and* ETERNAL LIFE**. (1 John 5:17-20)

***Keep yourselves in the love of God, looking for the mercy of our Lord Jesus Christ unto* ETERNAL LIFE.** And of some have *compassion*, making a difference: And *others save with fear*, pulling them out of the fire; hating even the garment spotted by the flesh. *Now unto him that is able to keep you from falling, and to present you faultless before the presence of his glory with exceeding joy,* To the only wise God our Saviour, be glory and majesty, dominion and power, both now and ever. Amen. (Jude 1:21-25)

CHAPTER 39

PARADISE

And one of the malefactors which were hanged railed on him, saying, If thou be Christ, save thyself and us. But the other answering rebuked him, saying, Dost not thou fear God, seeing thou art in the same condemnation? And we indeed justly; for we receive the due reward of our deeds: but this man hath done nothing amiss. And he said unto Jesus, **Lord, remember me when thou comest into thy kingdom. And Jesus said unto him, Verily I say unto thee, Today shalt thou be with me in PARADISE.** (Luke 23:39-43)

It is not expedient for me doubtless to glory. I will come to visions and revelations of the Lord. I knew a man in Christ above fourteen years ago, (whether in the body, I cannot tell; or whether out of the body, I cannot tell: God knoweth;) such an one caught up to the third heaven. And I knew such a man, (whether in the body, or out of the body, I cannot tell: God knoweth;) **How that he was caught up into PARADISE, and heard unspeakable words, which it is not lawful for a man to utter.** (2 Corinthians 12: 1-4)

He that hath an ear, let him hear what the Spirit saith unto the churches; ***To him that overcometh will I give to eat of the tree of life, which is in the midst of the* PARADISE *of God.*** (Revelation 2:7)

CHAPTER 40

VICTORY

That it might be fulfilled which was spoken by Esaias the prophet, saying, Behold my servant, whom I have chosen; my beloved, in whom my soul is well pleased: *I will put my spirit upon him,* and he shall shew judgment to the Gentiles. He shall not strive, nor cry; neither shall any man hear his voice in the streets. A bruised reed shall he not break, and smoking flax shall he not quench, **till he send forth judgment unto VICTORY**. And in his name shall the Gentiles trust. (Matthew 12:17-21)

And so it is written, The first man Adam was made a living soul; the last Adam was made a quickening spirit. Howbeit that was not *first* which is spiritual, but that which is *natural*; and *afterward* that which is *spiritual*. The first man is of the earth, earthy; the second man is the Lord from heaven. As is the earthy, such are they also that are earthy: and as is the heavenly, such are they also that are heavenly. And as we have borne the image of the earthy, we shall also bear the image of the heavenly. Now this I say, brethren, that flesh and blood cannot inherit the kingdom of God; neither doth corruption inherit incorruption. Behold, I shew you a mystery; We shall not all sleep, but we shall all be changed, In a moment, in the twinkling of an eye, at the last trump: for the trumpet shall sound, and the dead shall be raised incorruptible, and we shall be changed. *For this corruptible must put on incorruption, and this mortal must put on immortality.* So when this corruptible shall have put on incorruption, and this mortal shall have put on immortality, then shall be brought to pass the saying that is written, **Death is swallowed up in VICTORY. *O death, where is thy sting? O grave, where is thy* VICTORY?** The sting of death is sin; and the strength of sin is the law. ***But thanks be to God, which giveth us the* VICTORY *through our Lord Jesus Christ.*** Therefore, my beloved brethren, be ye stedfast, unmoveable, always abounding in the work of the Lord, forasmuch as ye know that your labour is not in vain in the Lord. (1 Corinthians 15:45-58)

Whosoever believeth that Jesus is the Christ is born of God: and every one that loveth him that begat loveth him also that is begotten of him. *By this we know that we love the children of God, when we <u>love God</u>, and <u>keep his commandments</u>.* For this is the love of God, that we keep his commandments: and his commandments are not grievous. ***For whatsoever is born of God <u>overcometh</u> the world: and this is the* VICTORY *that overcometh the world, even our faith.*** Who is he that overcometh the world, but he that believeth that Jesus is the Son of God? (1John 5:1-5)

And I saw as it were a sea of glass mingled with fire: and ***them that had gotten the* VICTORY *over the beast, and over his image, and over his <u>mark</u>,***

and over the number of his name, stand on the sea of glass, having the harps of God. And they sing the song of Moses the servant of God, and the song of the Lamb, saying, ***Great and marvellous are thy works, Lord God Almighty; just and true are thy ways, thou King of saints. Who shall not fear thee, O Lord, and glorify thy name? for thou only art holy: for all nations shall come and worship before thee; for thy judgments are made manifest.*** (Revelation 15:2-4)

Bibliography

The King James Bible

www.ingramcontent.com/pod-product-compliance
Lightning Source LLC
LaVergne TN
LVHW051040080426
835508LV00019B/1631